A NATION IN CRISIS

THE MELTDOWN OF MONEY, GOVERNMENT, AND RELIGION

★ ★ ★

A NATION IN CRISIS

THE MELTDOWN OF MONEY, GOVERNMENT, AND RELIGION

LARRY BATES & CHUCK BATES

FRONT LINE

A STRANG COMPANY

Most STRANG COMMUNICATIONS BOOK GROUP products are available at special quantity discounts for bulk purchase for sales promotions, premiums, fund-raising, and educational needs. For details, write Strang Communications Book Group, 600 Rinehart Road, Lake Mary, Florida 32746, or telephone (407) 333-0600.

A NATION IN CRISIS: THE MELTDOWN OF MONEY, GOVERNMENT, AND RELIGION
by Larry Bates and Chuck Bates
Published by FrontLine
A Strang Company
600 Rinehart Road
Lake Mary, Florida 32746
www.strangbookgroup.com

Unless otherwise noted, all Scripture quotations are from the New King James Version of the Bible. Copyright © 1979, 1980, 1982 by Thomas Nelson, Inc., publishers. Used by permission.

Scripture quotations marked KJV are from the King James Version of the Bible.

Cover design by Justin Evans
Design Director: Bill Johnson

Library of Congress Cataloging-in-Publication Data
Bates, Larry.
  A nation in crisis : the meltdown of money, government, and religion /
by Larry Bates and Chuck Bates. -- 1st ed.
      p. cm.
  Includes bibliographical references and index.
  ISBN 978-1-61638-148-6
  1. Economics--Religious aspects--Christianity. 2. Economics--United
States--History. 3. United States--Religion. 4. United
States--Economic conditions. 5. United States--Politics and government.
I. Bates, Chuck. II. Title.
  BR115.E3B36 2010
  261.8'50973--dc22

                            2010015772

10 11 12 13 14 — 9 8 7 6 5 4 3
Printed in the United States of America

CONTENTS

INTRODUCTION

MOST WOULD AGREE THAT OUR CURRENT ECONOMIC crisis did not occur overnight but, rather, has been building for many years. The majority of the controlled media has managed to paralyze the thinking of most people with a systematic program of disinformation that flows from an uninformed media, laden not only with intellectual incest but also with a propensity to be "in bed" with the financial, government, and religious establishments.

As we unpack the information contained in this book, we are guided by the words of Patrick Henry, one of the founders of our great nation, when he said, "It is natural for man to indulge in the illusions of hope. We are apt to shut our eyes against a painful truth and listen to the song of that siren 'til she transforms us into beasts. Is this the part of wise men, engaged in a great and arduous struggle for liberty? Are we disposed to be among the numbers of those who, having eyes, see not and having ears, hear not, the things which so nearly concern their temporal salvation? For my part, whatever anguish of spirit it may cost, I am willing to know the whole truth; to know the worst and to provide for it."[1]

In this book, we will unravel the confusion and unmask the mystery surrounding the institutions controlling our money, our government, and our religions. We will also offer strategies and solutions for these difficult times.

This is a worldwide mess, and there is something very sinister behind it. In this book, we will reveal to you what is really going on. It is far bigger than, and beyond the ability of, any government to resolve. More often than not, governments are at the heart of the problem, and most of their actions only serve to exacerbate the problem. You will be shocked to know that our current economic meltdown is being caused by five powerful, dangerous, and unstoppable forces: (1) a major banking crisis, (2) federal debt and deficits, (3) business and personal loans, (4) recession and depression, and (5) major inflation. You are not being fully informed by Wall Street or government officials, and most of the media are only repeating what the politicians and bankers tell them.

We will help you separate yourself from the masses who are now—or soon will be—the victims of this worldwide debacle. We are not "doom and gloomers"; we really believe you can not only position yourself for great financial opportunity, but you can also get your family and yourself out of harm's way and turn the chaos into blessing for yourself and others.

Each chapter will help you understand what you are dealing with and how the system really works. We will show you how we believe all of this will play out. We will also show you why this crisis occurred. with this information, you will be able to "connect the dots" and know how to defend those around you and yourself.

When you know what and who is behind this debacle and how the so-called "system" works, you will be ahead of the crowd. This is not just a recent scheme hatched by evil men. It has been in the works for centuries and is even predicted throughout the Bible. Time is running short, and the crisis is only beginning to unfold. Very soon, a lot of people will be asking, "Why didn't anyone see this coming?" and "Why didn't anyone warn us?" Now you won't have to be one of those people.

Our writing and analysis come from our backgrounds in economics, banking, and government, and as news executives and from our study of the Bible.

PART 1
MONEY

CHAPTER 1

MOST WON'T SAY IT, BUT YOU SHOULD KNOW

The Truth Behind Our Monetary, Political, and Religious Systems

By Larry Bates

IN THE SUMMER OF 2009, WHILE TAPING A TELEVISION program in Branson, Missouri, I was approached by a member of the studio audience by the name of Mr. Tolliver, who told me a story about a smart parrot who was not "politically correct."

According to the story, a favorite tourist shop had the famed parrot perched at the front of the store, and the parrot would greet each customer with whatever was on his mind. One day, a rough-looking character walked in, and the parrot took a look at the man and squawked, "You are the ugliest man I have ever seen!" Greatly offended, the customer complained to the store manager, who promptly grabbed the parrot, took him out back, and roughed him up, hoping to teach him some manners that were more "politically correct." The duly chastened parrot was placed back on his perch. In a little while, the offended customer prepared to leave the store, and as he walked past the parrot, the bird eyed him and said, "I can't say it... *but you know!*"

Many people know and understand truth but are afraid to say it for fear of being "roughed up" by the politically correct crowd in the media, government, and various institutions. I am reminded of a well-known passage in the Bible: "And ye shall know the truth, and the truth shall make you free" (John 8:32, KJV). Without truth, we are all in bondage to what we don't know or don't understand.

The single factor that contributes most to our current crisis is the failure or outright refusal to face facts. Facts are truly stubborn things, and they just don't go away, regardless of our refusal to face them or our attempts to manufacture our own set of facts.

If we are to survive as a nation, or even survive as a civilized people, we must raise up wisdom in a generation that lacks wisdom. We believe that wisdom will come from "iron sharpening"—a frank discussion of issues and events that affect us all. In this chapter, we will encapsulate some of the critical issues facing us now that are but examples of how deep and critical the crisis has become. Most traditional assumptions and expectations about money, government, and religion have been—or are about to be—blown apart. Life as we have known it in the United States is about to change, and change drastically; the one thing that will separate you from the masses is knowledge...knowledge of how the system works and the players involved.

Beginning of Our Problems

Our problems began in the Garden of Eden with the two players (Adam and Eve) that God had created and placed in paradise. Because of disobedience (sin), we (Adam and all his descendants) got kicked out of the garden, and paradise ended. The "free lunch" was over. Man had to go to work. However, labor is pain, and man's nature is to try to avoid pain.

The Origin of Plunder

Frédéric Bastiat, an economist and deputy in the French Assembly, wrote a book near the end of his life titled *The Law*. It is the second best book I have ever read—second only to the Bible. In *The Law*, Bastiat says, "Man can live and satisfy his wants only by cease-less labor, by the ceaseless application of his faculties to natural resources. This process is the origin of property. But it is also true that a man may live and satisfy his wants by seizing and consuming the products of the labor of others. This process is the origin of Plunder."[1]

We now use even government itself and the force of law to plunder. For example, if I hold a gun to your head and demand you empty your wallet or purse and give me the contents, I can go to jail under the laws of any state in the country. However, send me to Congress where I pass a law that empties your wallets and purses and I will probably get plenty of support—from those to whom I gave your money! Stealing is stealing, regardless of what we call it. We've just gotten more sophisticated in our stealing. Most of the media glorify it, and many in the religious camp even bless the plunder in the name of "social justice." It's kind of like putting lipstick on a pig—the pig may look a lot nicer, but it is still a pig.

We Were Warned

Alexander Fraser Tyler, a British professor over two hundred years ago, warned of how to create an economic crisis. You see, Tyler knew that a republic (rule by law) protects life, liberty, and property. He also knew that a democracy was a temporary and transitional government on its way to totalitarian government. In fact, it was Professor Tyler who stated, "A democracy can last as long and until a majority of its citizens discover they can vote them-selves largesse (large gifts) out of the public treasury, and they will continue to elect the politician promising the most; the end result is a fall of that democracy due to economic ruin and chaos."[2]

In 1797, George Washington, the first president of our republic, said, "Government is not reason. It is not eloquence. Government is force; like fire, it is a dangerous servant and a fearful master."

Recently we have witnessed the national debate over government-run health care—which has nothing to do with health care and everything to do with controlling the economic and social behavior of everyone. That aside, let's look at government's track record in running anything. The following is a (partial) list of functions and government-run programs and their degree of success or failure.

FUNCTION, PROGRAM, GOVERNMENT-RUN ENTERPRISE	STATUS
Postal service	Broke
Social security	Broke
Medicare	Broke
Medicaid for the poor	Broke
Amtrak	Broke
FDIC	Broke

In short, government has broken everything it has ever tried to manage. Government has NO money that it first did not take from someone else. As an example, let's see how they plan to fund this new health care reform program. A word search of the 2,074-page "healthcare reform bill," H.R. 3590, reveals that the word *tax* is used 183 times, *taxable* 164 times, *excise tax* 8 times, *taxes* 17 times, *fee* 152 times, *penalty* 115 times, *require* 166 times, *must* 45 times, and *shall* 3,607 times.

So, what does all of this mean to you? It means that you don't have much say over your own health care, and you "shall" do what the government says—*3,607 times.*

A New Financial Crisis?

"The U.S. must fix its growing debt problems or risk a new financial crisis," warned Thomas Hoenig, president of the Federal Reserve Bank of Kansas City, adding, "a mounting deficit could spur inflation. Without pre-emptive action, the U.S risks its next crisis."[3]

In fact, the government's (Obama's) economic plan to date is a recipe for disaster—particularly, disaster for most investments, as it will cripple the equity markets for years to come, stifle any economic recovery, and bring back massive double-digit inflation. Let's look at the Obama record:

1. $825 billion for President Obama's so-called "stimulus" package

2. Obama's record-breaking, near-$4 trillion federal budget

3. $100 billion to Fannie Mae and Freddie Mac, the home loan banks, and almost $500 billion of mortgage-backed securities guaranteed by Fannie Mae, Freddie Mac, and Ginnie Mae

4. $37 billion to continuing bailouts for GM and Chrysler

5. $750 billion to bail out the financial sector

6. $140 billion to bail out AIG insurance group

7. Untold number of promises to guarantee bailout of malinvestment by almost every sector of society

8. Then, there is the so-called "health care" package proposed by Obama that puts 7 percent of Americans on a government subsidy to help pay for the mandatory insurance, and raises taxes on 25 percent of those earning under $200,000 a year. It also raises taxes on three out of every four middle-class families in order to pay for each family receiving the government subsidy. Further, Obamacare taxes and

hurts seniors by taking $500 billion from Medicare,
which is also in financial trouble. In a time when
many people are struggling and we are trying to
shore up our fragile economy, why are we punishing
middle-class families with higher taxes?

For *each $50 billion* in government expenditures, the share for
the average family of four is $700. Since only half of the families of
four actually pay taxes, we have to double the figure—so the obligation of the average taxpaying family of four is now $1,400. Translated,
this means that, for every *$1 trillion* in government spending, the
average taxpaying family of four now is obligated for $28,000!

Who Benefits?

So, who benefits from all of this government largesse? Chris W.
Bell, who is himself a black man, wrote for *The American Thinker:*
"For the last seventy years, liberals have asked blacks to elect and
empower them so they could defend us (blacks) from racist conservatives who were trying to keep us down. They said without them,
we would be relegated to an inferior education, lower-paying jobs
and the sorrow of institutional racism. (And it has happened, but
with a different cause.) But after all this time in power, how has
liberalism benefited us?"[4]

Bell goes on to say, "Black America is in a state of crisis, and not
only are we being ignored by those for whom we vote, but we are
also being ignored by the press and the 'civil rights movement.'" He
asks, "When was the last time you heard anyone express outrage
over the fact that up to half of the black kids in major cities are high
school dropouts?"[5]

The black unemployment rate, Bell states, is higher than the
white rate: 8.7 percent for whites, versus 16.5 percent (90 percent
higher, based on Bell's figures [editor]). All this, he points out, is
after several decades of a solid black vote for liberals and socialists.

Chris Bell writes, "At each election, liberals say blacks need protection from conservatives, but there are no conservatives anywhere near us. The only thing that all of the people who set the policies that affect us have in common is that they are all liberal. Our cities have been under liberal control for decades, and they (the cities) are also where the black economic and social indicators are the worst and the mainstream civil rights movement that claims to represent us never questions whether or not liberalism is partially to blame."[6]

The inner cities are a mess, as they have higher taxes, more serious crime, and slow police response—all of which result in higher costs to businesses in the area. Capital flees, and those remaining are saddled with higher taxes, more regulatory oversight at every level, and generally deteriorating conditions that foster no economic activity until the next government-sponsored urban renewal program comes along.

The social implications are even worse, as more than 70 percent of black women give birth out of wedlock.[7] In the seventies, liberals told us that we didn't need marriage to enjoy our sexuality. One feminist even stated, "Women need men like a fish needs a bicycle." Liberals had more influence over the black community than the white community because they provided the black community government "mentors" who encouraged black women not to consider marriage as a prerequisite for having children; as a result, we have millions of single women trying to earn a living, raise kids, and run the household alone.

As Bell stated, "King had a dream, but blacks now face a nightmare."

Economic Bright Spot

The number of federal workers earning six-figure salaries has exploded during the recession, according to a *USA Today* analysis of government workers' pay. The paper reports, "Federal employees making salaries of $100,000 or more jumped from 14 percent to 17 percent of civil servants during the recession's first 18 months, and that's before overtime pay and bonuses are counted. Federal workers are enjoying an extraordinary boom time—both in pay and in hiring—during a recession that has cost 7.3 million jobs in the private sector."[8]

The average federal worker now makes $71,206, according to the Office of Personnel Management, while the average private sector wage is $40,331. That's roughly a $30,000 difference, and we are all paying for it. According to the USA Today analysis, in one department when the boss got a raise from Congress, other workers did too. "When the Federal Aviation Administration (FAA) chief's salary rose, nearly 1,700 employees had their salaries lifted above $170,000 too."[9]

Not-So-Bright Spot

The U.S. government statistics are being reported as a positive indicator that the U.S. economy is rebounding from a severe recession. However, we are hearing contradictory data from across America. In fact, most serious students of the economy put little stock in government data, as it has proven to be somewhat unreliable. One report we watch is the Ceridian-UCLA Pulse of Commerce Index. This index tracks truckers who are hauling goods across the country with their big rigs. By measuring fill-ups at more than seven thousand truck stops across America, the index monitors the flow of goods across the country and is an indication of U.S. economic output. The trucker index fell at a 36.8 percent annual rate in January 2010 after soaring 60.8 percent in December. The index's less volatile three-month moving average fell to 3.3 percent annual growth in January, from 14.6 percent in December 2009.[10]

These findings show that the celebrated 5.7 percent annual

growth rate the government reported for the fourth quarter of 2009 is probably not accurate and will have to be revised. *USA Today* reports, "Ceridian provides the corporate cards that thousands of truckers use to buy diesel. So it monitors fuel purchases as they are made—a real-time peek into the nationwide movement of commerce and one that doesn't require the revisions that plague other economic indicators."[11]

The Hard Truth

As economists, we have come to the stark realization that the Obama administration and Democratic leaders in Congress either don't know what they are doing or they know *precisely* what they are doing—either way, they are destroying our country.

Economist Arthur B. Laffer, former chief economist at the Office of Management and Budget (OMB) and a member of President Ronald Reagan's Economic Policy Advisory Board, says President Barack Obama's proposed budget "is the perfect plan for catastrophe, as it shows no spending restraint and raises tax rates."[12]

Laffer said the blueprint under Obama puts a greater burden on people who work and gives more money to people who don't, stating, "If you tax people who work and pay people who don't, do not be surprised if you find a lot of people not working. If you tax rich people and give the money to poor people, you're going to have lots and lots of poor people and no rich people."[13]

Most people view the American dream as the chance for the poor to become rich without making the rich poor. One key thing Laffer points out is, "If you have two locations with different tax rates, producers and manufacturers will move to the locale with lower rates; and Obama's [plans] take no account whatsoever of the effect this will have on global competitiveness and the creation of jobs in the United States."[14]

Former House Majority Leader Dick Armey (R-TX) described

for us in an interview (spring 2008) how the Democratic Party is the "academic party" that must use iconic images rather than real thought and analysis to advance their agenda. He suggested that as a result, the Democrats, by taking this academic approach, will almost always advance their least accomplished members to leadership. Arthur Laffer confirmed this when he described Obama's somewhat academic approach to the economy, stating, "It's a classic professorial response: In the classroom, you never have skin in the game and you're never held accountable for your pronouncements. And that's exactly what's going on here."[15]

A friend of ours told us about an economics professor at a local college who was being confronted by students who had just come from the social science department, where they were being indoctrinated by their socialist professors. The professor stated that he had never failed a single student but had once failed an entire class. That class had insisted that Obama's socialism worked, and that no one would be rich and no one would be poor. In other words, Obamanomics would prove to be the "great equalizer." The professor announced a plan in his class that would experiment with Obama's plan, stating that all grades would be averaged and everyone would receive the same grade. No one would fail, and no one would receive an A.

After the first test, the grades were averaged and everyone got a B. The students who worked and studied hard were very upset, but the students who studied little or not at all were very happy. As the second test came along, the students who had studied little had studied even less, and the ones who had previously studied had studied very little. The second test average was a D, and *nobody* was happy. When the third test rolled around, the average was an F.

The professor reported that the test scores never increased, as the blame game, name-calling, and bickering all resulted in hard feelings, and no one was willing to study for the benefit of anyone else. All failed the class, to their great shock and surprise. The professor defended his actions by explaining that socialism would ultimately always fail because when the reward is great, the effort to succeed is great; but when government takes all the reward away, there will be no incentive for anyone to make the effort to succeed. My good friend, the late Adrian Rogers, who pastored Bellevue Baptist Church in Memphis, always reminded me, "You cannot multiply wealth by dividing it." That is still true today.

Green and Godless

A few years ago, I saw a disturbing trend where a major push was being made to convince the masses to surrender all sanity and embrace without question or discussion the theory of "global warming" with all its required personal sacrifices and massively increased taxes. While attending a meeting of the Fort Collins, Colorado, Rotary Club, I had the opportunity to hear the guest speaker that day, who was none other than Dr. William Gray, the celebrated climatologist at Colorado State University and CNN's preeminent hurricane forecaster. When the meeting opened the floor for questions, I went to the microphone and asked Dr. Gray, "Is the global warming theory based on real science—or junk science?" I will never forget his answer. He said, "You need to ask a political scientist, as it has nothing to do with science."

On April 27, 2007, I observed a Bloomberg Wire Service story that stated, "Visitors to the Gala Napa Valley Hotel and Spa won't find the Gideon Bible in the nightstand drawer. Instead, on the bureau will be a copy of *An Inconvenient Truth*, former vice president Al Gore's book about global warming. They will also find the Gala equipped with waterless urinals, solar lighting, and recycled paper as it marches toward becoming California's first hotel certified as 'green,' or benevolent to the environment."[16]

Now, don't get me wrong—I am for good stewardship of the natural resources God has entrusted to us; I just don't worship them.

In fact, we installed geothermal heating and cooling in our home because it was an economical way to save energy and money.

Islam and the West

In addition to the systematic meltdown of our economy and political structure, we face an enemy that is intent on *jihad* ("holy war") with the United States, Israel, and the entire Western world. Islam is intent on total world domination under sharia law, which includes government and finance.

A former intelligence officer explained to me that all of Islam is intent on world domination and that there are three types of Muslims:

- Type 1: The revolutionary—one who will strap on a bomb, have someone else do the bombing, or plant an IED (improvised explosive device) in order to intimidate their target (Western values) into submission

- Type 2: The evolutionary—one who also believes in world domination under Islamic (sharia) law, but believes it will be accomplished by breeding and propaganda

- Type 3: The westernized (peaceful) Muslim—one who loves Western values and has a job and family. However, one day a type 1 Muslim knocks on type 3 Muslim's door. Let's say type 3 is a computer expert and is asked to help take down the infidels' (our) computer systems. He refuses and is threatened with the kidnapping, rape, and killing of his wife and the taking of his children. Further, his family in the Middle East is threatened. What do you think

type 3 Muslim will do? A recent Pew Research
poll found, in fact, that one in four younger U.S.
Muslims are OK with homicide bombings against
innocent civilians.[17]

Further, radical Islam is intent on making sharia finance the next global financial system. It seeks to undermine and convert competitive Western capitalism into a monopolistic sharia system by infiltrating our institutions from within. We have even seen major financial institutions like HSBC Bank, Citigroup, Charles Schwab, AIG, and others announce that some divisions will offer sharia-compliant banking, where a committee of sheikhs will decide the economic activities to be sanctioned by the Islamists. I have to conclude that Islam is nothing but communism with a religious label.

Most Won't Touch This One

The American Left has a habit of trying to smear its critics with labels such as "tea bagger" and "birther." The term "birther" was applied to those who questioned Barack Obama's eligibility to be president of the United States under the constitutional requirement that to be eligible one must be a natural-born citizen of the United States.

We interviewed the celebrated author, columnist, and writer for the *Washington Times*, Amanda Carpenter, on the national news magazine *News & Views* on September 30, 2009. Carpenter, who is considered by many to be a "conservative" writer, was asked by both of us during the live interview about Obama's Muslim and socialist leanings. We even asked her about the "natural-born" qualification issue, to which she quickly proclaimed, "He is qualified. I have seen the birth certificate." I responded, "If you have seen it, you are the only person I know who has seen it!" Ms. Carpenter, not wanting to get into this discussion, quickly ended the interview. As we say in the media, "She cut and ran."

So, what are the facts? Is he or isn't he (Obama) a natural-born citizen, qualified to be president? What most people know is the Associated Press (AP) is one of the largest internationally recognized, syndicated news services. In fact, our broadcast company is a member of the AP Press Association. What most people do *not* know is that in 2004, the AP was a "birther" news organization. In a syndicated report, published Sunday, June 27, 2004, by the *Kenyan Standard Times*, the AP reporter stated in his story, "Kenyan-born U.S. Senate hopeful Barack Obama appeared set to take over the Illinois Senate seat after his main rival, Jack Ryan, dropped out of the race on Friday night amid a furor over lurid sex club allegations."[18] A photocopy of the newspaper article appearing in Kenya's largest Sunday newspaper, the *Kenyan Sunday Standard* on June 27, 2004, backs up the AP story with the headline, "Kenyan-born Obama All Set for U.S. Senate."[19]

This report explains the context of the often-cited debate between Obama and former U.S. ambassador to the United Nations, Alan Keyes, Obama's opponent for the Senate seat. In the debates during the fall of 2004, Keyes would fault Obama for not being a "natural-born citizen" and for Obama's quick retort, "So what? I'm running for Illinois senator, not the presidency."[20]

Maybe it's "buyer's remorse," but many seem to be waking up to the activities and policies of Barack Obama, who seems intent on installing an America never seen before. Economist, lawyer, writer, and actor Ben Stein says in his column in *The American Spectator*, "Now the American people are starting to wake up to the truth. Barack Obama is a super-likeable, super-Leftist, not a fan of this country, way, way too cozy with the terrorist leaders in the Middle East, way beyond naiveté, all the way into active destruction of our interests, our allies, and our future."[21]

Religion or Relationship

Many will be shocked to read that the root word of *religion* is *religio*, which means "to return to bondage."[22] I describe religion as man's attempt to reach God on man's terms and conditions. It is ritual without righteousness, form without force. It cannot refresh you, and it cannot change you. Jesus Christ is God's attempt to reach man with His grace, His love, and His mercy.

A recent news shocker was a statement by the Vatican's chief exorcist, who stated, "The devil is in the Vatican."[23] Father Gabriele Amorth, who is eighty-five and has been the Vatican's chief exorcist for twenty-five years and claims to have dealt with over seventy thousand cases of demonic possession, says sex-abuse scandals in the Roman Catholic Church are proof that "the devil is at work inside the Vatican."[24] Don Gabriele Amorth cites the consequences of satanic infiltration, which include power struggles at the Vatican, "cardinals who do not believe in Jesus, and bishops who are linked to the demon."[25]

Even in evangelical churches, we see a "seeker-friendly" doctrine being taught and preached. Entertainment is as big as the mortgages on many of the super structures called churches today. There has developed a real competition for the "sheep," and many have watered down the gospel in order to attract them.

In reality, the gospel is the powerful, all-encompassing message of God's kingdom principles, given to provide wisdom and guidance in all things, whether it be matters of spiritual growth or wisdom in areas such as economics or politics. Again, each of us has been called to raise up wisdom in a generation that lacks wisdom. It is our hope that the chapters that follow will give real insight to the inner workings of our financial, political, and religious systems and help you and those around you develop strategies and prepare for the coming collapse.

CHAPTER 2

MONEY ANSWERETH ALL THINGS

Understanding Our Monetary System

By Larry Bates

W E'VE ALL READ AND HEARD OF WHAT WAS TERMED the "economic crisis" in Asia. Question: Was it purely an economic crisis, or was it a crisis of just a component of the economy? The facts show that there did not exist a general economic crisis in Asia; there was a currency crisis.

How so? Let's take the country of Indonesia as an example. This is the fourth most populated country in the world. I've visited Indonesia many times, and I can tell you firsthand that Indonesia is a very wealthy country. It is an OPEC member, with vast oil and gas reserves. Indonesia is rich with coal, timber, minerals, and agricultural resources. It has a huge labor force that works very cheaply. So what's the problem?

The problem centered around a currency crisis—a crisis of confidence in various currencies in Asia, including the Indonesian rupiah. We must view all paper currencies as merely "boats" hauling value for goods and services on the ocean of the economy, and all the boats are sinking. Some currency boats just happen to be sinking faster than others.

What Is Money?

What is money? Most people would answer, "It's what I have in my wallet or purse," or, "It's what I have in my bank account, or what I have in my brokerage money fund account," or a combination of these.

I must tell you that your understanding of money—or your lack of understanding—can mean either great fortune or great loss to you. Knowledge of our economic and monetary system is one thing that will determine whether you are one of the winners or one of the losers. John 8:32 reads, "And you shall know the truth, and the truth shall make you free." It's not the truth that's going to make you free, but it's your *knowledge* of the truth. We have a choice to either be good stewards of what God has given us by knowing the truth, or to just ignore the truth.

Money by Definition

The common definition that we find for *money* in the dictionary is as follows: (1) standard pieces of gold, silver, copper, nickel, etc., stamped by government authority and used as a medium of exchange and measure of value: coin or coins; also called hard money, and (2) any paper notes issued by a government or an authorized bank and used in the same way; bank notes; bills: also called paper money.[1]

We must examine the question, "What did we do before we had money?" The answer is: barter. Suppose that I'm a grain farmer. John is a dairy farmer, and Ben doesn't farm, but he owns a processing plant. I get tired of eating grain all the time, and I'd like to have some meat and some milk. John gets tired of drinking milk and eating meat, and Ben, who has the processing plant, would like something to eat. What do we do? I send grain to Ben and John, swapping for meat, milk, and the services of the processing plant.

In other words, all of us in our little economic units either produced goods as John and I did, or provided a service as Ben did.

But as we became a more mobile society, it became very difficult to pick up the grain and carry it everywhere to use as "money." It was more difficult for John to carry his cows, and it was impossible for Ben to pick up and move his processing plant around the country. So, what happened was the evolution of money. We saw money take on required characteristics in order to be considered money.

Money had to be something that everyone would accept in trade for various goods and services, and that could later be exchanged with someone else for goods and services that they needed. This key concept of a portable medium of exchange gave a great boost to trading and other economic activities. Money had become the medium, or the middleman, of all transactions, including investments, making trade and commerce more convenient.

We see throughout the history of early civilization that the increasing trade in commerce caused people to gravitate to gold and silver as the trading medium. We see in the early days of the Bible that gold and silver had great value. People had long desired the precious metals for jewelry and decoration. It was valuable because it took labor to prospect for it, it took labor to mine it, and it took labor to refine it. It represented one's labor and enterprise.

As time passed, a substance called electrum came into existence. Electrum was simply a mixture of gold and silver, molded into a crude ball or lump. These lumps of electrum were used as the medium of exchange because everyone knew from experience these lumps would not lose their value. It was widely recognized as money, and change could be made by shaving off pieces of electrum until the proper weight for payment had been achieved.

After electrum, in its crude form, we saw the advent of coinage around 650 B.C. People still liked electrum, but coins were far better. Coins were pre-weighted and had different sizes and denominations. It was not necessary to shave off the pieces to make change.

With the advent of coinage, man's sinful nature rose up again. Kings and governments discovered a powerful secret: They could give themselves a monopoly of the mint by simply decreeing that only coins authorized by the king could be used. The "official" character of coins was further enhanced when the king put his image on the coins.

By controlling the minting of coins, it also became easy for the king (or the government) to steal from the people by simply debasing the coins. He did that by periodically calling in all the coins of the realm. He would then melt them, add a small amount of cheap base metal to the gold or silver, then remint them. Because he had added the base metal, he had more coins than before. They were still accepted at face value by the people when the king first spent them, because they didn't know any better. This is much like what is happening today, but in a far more sophisticated way.

This had become a "back-door" tax on the people. How? It's simple. The one who gets the new money first, or who knows about the new money first, profits at the expense of the one who gets it last or knows about it last. You see, the king had a definite advantage because he got to spend the money first. Many times, the king would create more coins to finance his wars or to bestow gifts upon his subjects.

The most insidious thing about this back-door tax is the fact that the people didn't even know they were being taxed. That, my friends, is fraud. Even back in the prophet Amos's day, we read that they made "the ephah [bushel] small, and the shekel [dollar] great…falsifying the balances by deceit" (Amos 8:5, KJV).

Banks Are Born

As early civilization advanced and trade and commerce boomed, and with coins being cumbersome and heavy to carry around, someone decided we should have banks where we could deposit our coins for safekeeping. A depository receipt was given, showing how many coins the individual had on deposit. Soon, it became evident that it was far easier to transport the depository receipts than the actual coins, and since the bankers would redeem the depository receipts and return the coins to the person presenting the receipt, it became commonplace to trade the receipts rather than the coins. Thus, paper money came into existence.

The king then discovered that he could do exactly the same thing with paper money that he had done with gold. He printed pieces of paper that represented the quantity of gold or silver that he had in the royal treasury. Then, by decree, he made it illegal to use anything except his paper money (legal tender laws).

The Fraud

Over time, the king gradually severed the relationship between the quantity of paper and the quantity of gold and silver in the royal treasury until the paper was based on nothing but the good faith and credit of the king. After all, the legal tender laws declared you had to use the king's money.

As more and more money was created, it became more plentiful. And as it became more plentiful, it had a diminished value. This is what we know today as inflation.

If we go to the dictionary for the definition of *inflation*, we read: (1) an inflating or being inflated, and (2) an increase in the amount of money and credit in relation to the supply of goods and services.[2]

Inflation is something like this: If I serve you a cup of black coffee and then start pouring clear hot water in your coffee to dilute it, and if your objective in drinking the coffee is the caffeine it contains, then you're going to have to drink a lot more coffee to get the same amount of caffeine. The same thing happens with our money. As we have more money printed and put into circulation, the result is a fall in its value and a rise in prices.

Real Money

You may be asking, "What should money be, then?" Money should be something that has all ten of the following characteristics. If it does, it will function as it should.

1. It should be a store of value. Your money should be worth, in terms of purchasing power, what it is worth today, next year, or even in ten years.

2. It should be easily recognizable as money. We can't expect someone to accept it as payment if they don't know what it is.

3. It should be universally acceptable. If people do not desire it, it has no value in trade.

4. It should be easily divisible. This is a must in order to make change.

5. It should have intrinsic value. It should be desirable in and of itself.

6. It should be impossible to counterfeit. If it cannot be counterfeited, it cannot be created out of nothing. If it cannot be created out of nothing, there can be no inflation and resulting depreciation in its value.

7. It should be durable. If it is not durable and deteriorates or is easily destroyed, its value will not last over time.

8. It should have high value in small quantities. A concentration of value or wealth makes it more convenient to transport.

9. It must be easy to handle. It must be in a size and form easy to store, transport, and exchange.

10. Its supply must remain scarce.

When we compare most of the paper currencies, including the U.S. Federal Reserve note (dollar), to this list, we find they have only a few of the ten characteristics. The U.S. Federal Reserve note has only three. Real money must have all ten. However, we must remember that people—not governments, central banks, or even nation states—have always determined what money is and what money is not.

In all of recorded history, including the Holy Bible, we have seen that the currency of choice and the money of the Bible is gold and silver. We read in 1 Kings 10:2 that when the queen of Sheba came to visit King Solomon, she came bearing gold and precious stones. (I cannot find anywhere in that text that she came bearing CDs and municipal bond portfolios.) This was the money of the day, and it has remained so for thousands of years, to this very day.

A Fatal Tendency

In biblical times and continuing to this very day, there always has been that sin nature of man and his fatal tendency to try to live and consume off the labor of others. The Babylonian monetary system is alive and well in the world today in the form of dishonest weights and measures. Our monetary system today is doing the very same thing that is mentioned in Amos 8:5. We are making the ephah (or bushel, or whatever quantity we're buying) smaller, and we are making the shekel (or dollar, as we know it today) larger by inflating it so that it buys less goods. Thus, we cheat with dishonest scales.

We must again remember that people—not governments, central banks, or even nation states—have always determined what money is and what money is not.

This is an abomination to almighty God. This is a system, a commercial Babylonian system, that He already has judged; it is a system that we as believers must come out of. It's really simple. When you don't totally use the king's (the government's) money, the king (the government) can't totally rip you off.

You don't need legal tender laws to tell people what money they should use. You only need legal tender laws when the money that is being used is not what the marketplace desires but what is being forced upon the people by the edict of the king or the decree of the government.

If one is to survive this coming economic disorder, one must learn what money is and what money is not. When people understand, there will be a mad rush to dump the counterfeit and grab the real thing.

Don't you think it's strange that the Federal Reserve (a private bank), who in 1913 was given a monopoly on the creation of paper money by "the king" (Congress and the president), has 35 to 40 percent of its real assets in gold?

We must remember that the gold at the Federal Reserve is not for our benefit. Nowhere on the Federal Reserve's notes that we carry around in our wallets does it say that they are redeemable for part of the gold. The bills we accept as money are simply IOUs of the Federal Reserve.

Try to find on the face of any Federal Reserve note what it owes you; you will find that it says it owes you nothing. Therefore, you are carrying around a pocket full of "IOU nothing" notes.

In effect, we've all said together, "Just forget the gold; give me the dollar."

I challenge you now to pull any bill out of your wallet and examine it carefully. If you have a one-dollar bill and you ask the average person on the street to identify this bill for you, they will, in most instances, say it is a dollar. I must tell you that it is not a dollar.

The word *dollar* comes from the Greek word *thaler,* which means "unit of measurement." Congress defined a dollar as so many grains of silver and later as so many grains of gold.

Suppose you saw me pick up a two-pound bag of coffee at the local supermarket. You were behind me in the checkout line as I said to the clerk, "Just pour out the coffee and give me the two pounds." What would you think? I know what you would think. You would think, "Wow, he's really lost it!" But that's exactly what you've done with your dollar.

This is precisely how the economic and political elite of this world have been able to accomplish the biggest Robin Hood theft of all times. They have simply taken from the ignorant and given it to themselves, the well informed.

You must be asking yourself right now, "What kind of system allows this kind of chicanery?" Easy—the one we have. Proof is in the exhibits, just below, where the language on the series 1950 Federal Reserve note (exhibit A) says, "This note is legal tender for all debts public and private, and is redeemable in lawful money at the United States Treasury or at any Federal Reserve Bank."

EXHIBIT A

EXHIBIT B

This must mean that the new bill (exhibit B) is unlawful money. The only question remaining is what action we'll take individually. Noah is perhaps our best example in Hebrews 11:7: "By faith Noah, being warned of God of things not seen as yet, moved with fear, prepared an ark to the saving of his house."

It's time to build your financial ark.

CHAPTER 3

"FAITH-BASED" MONEY

The Evils and Risks of Our Fiat Money System

By Larry Bates

A FEW YEARS AGO, I WAS A GUEST LECTURER AT A GRAD-
uate level economic symposium at a prominent university. During the lecture, I mentioned the name of Roger
Sherman, whereupon I received a lot of blank stares. I then asked,
"Who can tell me who Roger Sherman is?"

Not a single student raised his hand. I must remind you, these
were graduate students working on their master's and doctorate
degrees. I then asked the head of the school of economics to tell the
group who Roger Sherman was. I was able to read the lips of this
PhD economist in the back of the auditorium as he was saying, "I
don't know."

I then asked, "How many can tell me who Karl Marx or John
Maynard Keynes were?" Everyone knew who they were.

So, who was Roger Sherman?

The answer is, he was a delegate from Connecticut to the
Constitutional Convention of 1787 and was responsible for crafting
the economic section of the Constitution of the United States of
America. Wouldn't you think this is important to know and to
teach to the students in any school of economics?

Sherman, as a delegate to the Constitutional Convention, was
attempting to address the major problem of the economy of the

colonies in the late 1700s (and by the way, the major economic problem we face today), which he outlined in his work titled *A Caveat Against Injustice: An Inquiry Into the Evils of a Fluctuating Medium of Exchange.*[1]

The problem they faced was a fluctuating and perishable "money" (medium of exchange). Many were using perishable agricultural products to pay debts.

Let's say I owe you one thousand dollars, and let's say watermelons are going for around two dollars each. I bring you a truckload of five hundred watermelons and dump them in your front yard, and you then declare my debt to you is "paid." You can imagine the problems and difficulties surrounding such a system. In fact, the practice was creating economic instability and chaos.

Correcting the Problem

Sherman's work to correct the injustice and evil surrounding the practice culminated in the adoption of Article 1, Section 10 of the U.S. Constitution. This section reads in part, "No state shall...make anything but gold and silver coin a tender in payment of debts." Six months after the adoption of the Constitution, historical accounts showed increased revenues to the young government (without a tax hike), the moneyed people bringing their coin into circulation, and a general atmosphere of monetary prosperity, trade, and commerce.

Our young republic flourished and prospered under the monetary system of honest weights and measures. The prosperity lasted until the "banksters," prompted by Rothschild bankers, started getting more and more control of the monetary system. Mayer Rothschild is known to have commented, "Give me control of a nation's monetary system and I care not who writes their laws."[2]

The Federal Reserve Act of 1913 established our fiat currency system (money by decree) that has been the cause of every economic problem or crisis in the United States and around the world since its inception. By subsequent fiat (decree), the U.S. currency and all other paper currencies have been reduced to nothing more than "boats" on the "ocean" of the economy. They are all sinking, but some (like the U.S. dollar) are sinking faster than others.

Bad Architecture

Suppose you are tenants in a magnificent high-rise office building that has become the most desirable center of world trade and commerce. To your surprise, the co-architect of the building reveals in a public interview the flaws of the building and predicts the probable collapse of the structure. What would happen? There would be a mass exodus from the building. The next major press conference would be from the head of building codes and enforcement, announcing the condemnation of the building. So, what does this have to do with our money?

Surprise Revelation, but Not Much Press

I was surprised to see on the front page of the business section of the *Denver Post* the headline "Co-creator of the Euro Offers Terra." The article, by *Denver Post* business writer Aldo Svaldi, read, "A co-architect of the euro, Bernard Lietaer, will unveil a new global currency called the 'terra' next week in Denver as an antidote to a worsening economic slump. For Lietaer, alternatives need to be found to the current 'faith-based' money system or else the U.S., Europe, and the rest of the world risk following Japan down the path of economic stagnation."[3]

Commenting on the current U.S. strategy to revive its economy, Lietaer told the *Denver Post*, "Dropping interest rates and increasing the money supply have proven it doesn't work."[4]

"The Japanese have increased their money supply 30 percent a year and have dropped interest rates to 0 percent over 12 years without reviving their economy. Massive deficit spending, public works projects, and voucher programs have all failed to bring a lasting recovery to the world's second-largest economy," Lietaer said.[5]

The stunning part of all this is that Lietaer's statements got no press coverage outside Denver and IRN/USA News.

Major Risks

Is Lietaer flying below the radar screen of official thought of the banksters, or is he simply being ignored? I believe even the banksters are in a box (particularly Bernanke) and are simply watching what Lietaer and others come up with; then, they will move to control it. The terra will be no different from the euro or the dollar as long as it is fiat (by decree) in nature. The United States and Europe, because of socialist policies, are facing the greatest economic challenges in history. In the last twenty-five years, eighty-seven countries have gone through a major currency crisis. This equates to a big majority of all people in the world having gone through a monetary crisis at least once in their lifetimes.

Americans are living under the illusion that it can't happen here. We falsely perceive a system of stability. But it *is* happening—*now!* Even the IMF (International Monetary Fund) warned recently that the current U.S. twin deficits (budget and trade) are unsustainable. If we (the United States) did not control the IMF, we would be operating under strict IMF fiscal policies. Many economists have speculated that if the United States had to live under the rules that have been imposed on many South American countries, the United States would become a developing nation in a couple of decades. The problem is systemic. The United States' current fiscal situation is unsustainable, unfair to the working masses, and won't work.

Bottom Line

Unstable currency systems equal unstable governments. Unfortunately, President Bush and his advisers succumbed to the temptation to try to outspend the Democrats lest he and the Republicans be labeled as "uncaring." This largesse certainly did not satisfy the Democrats, who were lusting to be back in power. The Democrats continued to hammer away at President Bush's economic policies, while not one of the Democratic candidates for president had so much as a clue to how the current economic system works, or even should work. The current political battles under Obama and the ultimate results will yield an unstable political and economic environment that could lead to a run on the dollar.

The dollar is a "faith-based" currency because its value is totally dependent on the ability of monetary policy makers and manipulators to keep the currency where anybody accepts it. Will you and millions of others around the world continue with your faith in their ability?

What's at Risk?

What you need to understand most about the coming collapse is that all of your dollar assets such as CDs, money funds, T-bills, annuities, and other paper assets are at great risk. Let's connect the dots. If the co-architect of the euro is concerned about the euro's lasting value, what does this mean for the U.S. dollar?

A few years ago, a client of our economic and political consulting group called and asked his economist to help facilitate the sale of all his precious metals holdings. When asked why one would want to dispose of precious metals now, the client replied, "A financial adviser said they are not doing anything, so get rid of them and let's put the proceeds in mutual funds."

To make an important point, the economist responded, "While you are at it, why don't you get rid of your homeowner's insurance, car insurance, health insurance, disability insurance, and any liability insurance, since they're probably not doing anything either."

The client responded, "I can't do that. I might get sick, have an accident, or my house could burn."

It is amazing that so many understand so little about risks to their assets and monetary holdings that can be brought about by changes in monetary policy, by natural disasters, and even terrorist acts. Former Federal Reserve Chairman Alan Greenspan said, "The Central Bank (Federal Reserve) must stand ready to deal with the large number of possible threats (risks) to the economy."[6]

Warren Buffet, the successful, world-famous investor, recently warned twenty thousand shareholders of his Berkshire Hathaway company about the dangers (risks) of looming inflation. Buffet confirmed that he had increased his bet against the U.S. dollar because of concerns over the record U.S. trade deficit. "Inflation is the enemy of the investor in terms of real returns," Buffet said.

On the risk of derivatives, Buffet said, "I would predict that some-time in the next ten years, we will have some very big problems (risks) accentuated by people's activities with derivatives." Buffet used the $6 billion accounting scandal with mortgage financier Freddie Mac to make his case for risks to the economy from derivatives. He noted they had "intelligent board members, were chartered by Congress, and monitored by a multitude of Wall Street analysts," but even these supposedly "smart" people could not get a handle on the complexity and risks in this market.

Buffet listed other risks:

1. "Auditors (large accounting firms) selling fraudulent tax shelters"

2. "Disgusting mutual fund managers playing with clients' assets to earn higher commissions"

3. "People getting terrible results from consulting the experts" (well-meaning financial advisers and planners who do not understand economic fundamentals)

4. "A checklist [used as a] substitute for thinking"

Understanding Risk

To understand all the risks involved with the economy and your assets, one must understand that economics is but human action, taken in the context of quantity of available money and credit and available goods and services in a given economic unit.

One must also understand that we have a debt-based, discretionary economy and monetary system.

Warren Buffet is absolutely correct when he says, "A checklist is no substitute for thinking." However, there is wisdom in using a checklist to ask questions to stimulate thinking. Here is our checklist:

- Do I understand what is meant by a debt-based economy and debt-based monetary system and how it affects me?

- Do I understand that the Federal Reserve is not federal and has doubtful reserves and, in fact, is a private bank that was given a monopoly on the creation of U.S. currency in 1913?

- Do I understand how the banking system really works—what money is and is not—and that people, not governments, central banks, or nation states, ultimately determine what money is? If not, or if you need to refresh your understanding, reread chapter 2.

- Do I understand there are two main categories of assets—ownership assets and loanership assets?

- Do I understand that in periods of economic and political uncertainty, I should move from less liquid to more liquid assets for the purpose of mobility and portability?

- Do I understand that in periods of a depreciating currency (i.e., dollar losing value against other currencies) one should move more assets from the "loanership" category to the "ownership" category to preserve asset value?

- Do I understand how election uncertainty and post-election economic policies will affect my tax burden and the value of my asset holdings?

- If the bulk of my assets is in real estate, do I understand how interest rate hikes will affect real estate values?

- Do I understand that with a rise in mortgage rates, and stricter lending practices, fewer people are qualifying for loans, and, therefore, fewer parcels of real estate are being sold?

- Do I know the condition of the bank to whom I've loaned (deposited) my money?

- Do I understand that if foreign investors lose their appetite for U.S. assets, the U.S. dollar will depreciate further?

- Do I understand how natural disasters will affect my asset holdings?

- Do I understand how one or more terrorist attacks on U.S. soil will affect markets and my assets?

- Do I fully understand my economic and political risks in the following list of assets?

OWNERSHIP ASSETS	LOANERSHIP ASSETS
Gold	Federal Reserve notes (paper currency)
Silver	Money market funds
Platinum	CDs
Rare coins	Treasury bills
Stocks	Annuities
Real estate	Bonds
Collectibles	Notes

The Truth About Inflation

With the calamitous debt that has been loaded onto the U.S. economy in less than two years as a result of irresponsible governance at all levels, the American people are hearing almost daily about the possible double-digit inflation that many economists say is sure to engulf us in the years just ahead.

As an abstract concept, the matter of inflation probably does not impact the "man on the street" as starkly as it should. Most view it as a cyclical phenomenon of the economy that comes and goes—in some ways like changes in the weather. But inflation is a far more serious matter. Inflation is a powerful, calculated method of *theft*, and it has been used for centuries by tyrants, dictators, kings, and yes—even our own U.S. government.

In fact, we can probably expect the inflation "tax" to be much greater than the direct tax from the government.

Simply put, inflation is an increase in credit and the money supply—and the chief result is soaring prices. As government increases the money supply by printing more money, the unit of exchange (dollar) loses value, and we find we cannot buy as much with our dollars as we did last year...or last month...or last week. In periods of catastrophic inflation seen in the past in many parts of the world, we saw the existing basis of society overturned where one day people had money that had value, and the next day they did not. Most credible economists around the world understand that inflation is the inevitable result of governments printing an oversupply of devalued currency. The harder prediction is precisely when it will hit.

If we use the word *inflation* to mean just rising prices, we have missed a key point: *inflation is* caused *by government monetary policies.* To narrow the point even further, *inflation is caused* solely *by the government printing more money.*

The obvious question, then, is why a government would deliberately print or have the privately owned central bank (Federal Reserve), to which it gave a monopoly of the mint, print an oversupply of money. The answer is simple: A government prints more money when the budget is out of balance. In other words, the government's expenditures have been excessive, it has run out of things to tax, it can't get anyone to loan it money, and as a result, it can't pay its bills.

And why does a government spend "excessively"? Again, there is a simple answer: Excessive expenditures, for the most part, are a result of redistribution of wealth and income. In other words, laws are passed—for political reasons—that force the productive members of society to support the unproductive.

Politicians would like us to believe that the causes of inflation are "multiple and complex." That's baloney. Let me say it again: *inflation is caused by printing too much money.*

When politicians and bureaucrats in government tinker around with the economy, there will invariably be trouble. Price controls, for example, cannot stop or even slow down inflation. Henry Hazlitt, a brilliant journalist and economist of the twentieth century whose thinking and writing fell within the Austrian tradition of Ludwig von Mises and F. A. Hayek, stated over thirty years ago:

> Price controls simply squeeze or wipe out profit margins, disrupt production, and lead to bottlenecks and shortages. All government price and wage controls, or even "monitoring," is merely an attempt by the politicians to shift the blame for inflation on to producers and sellers instead of their own monetary policies.[7]

Contrary to Keynesian economic theory, prolonged inflation does not "stimulate" the economy. In fact, it unbalances and disrupts the economy through inflated wages, inflated cost of materials, costlier benefits, and other increased costs too numerous to list that in turn suppress production and employment.

Henry Hazlitt also pointed out:

> Unemployment is mainly caused by excessive wage rates in some industries, brought about either by extortionate union demands, by minimum-wage laws (which keep teenagers and the unskilled out of jobs), or by prolonged and over-generous unemployment insurance.[8]

Do you recognize any of these factors in our current economic crisis?

What's the answer? It's the answer that politicians, especially on the Left, do not want to hear. It's not new, and it's not complicated:

- Understand that higher taxes are not the answer.
- Balance the budget.
- Stop reckless spending.

CHAPTER 4

THE COMING FINANCIAL WIPEOUT

How and When Will It Occur?

By Larry Bates

T HE BAD NEWS IS, WE FIND OURSELVES IN A PERILOUS economic fix due to factors we had no control over and probably never participated in. However, the good news is that in periods of economic turbulence, downturns, or outright economic collapse, wealth is not destroyed (except in cases of civil disorder, riots, etc.) but is simply transferred. Money is the transfer agent.

System Problems

Our current financial predicament could only occur in a debt-based economic system and a debt-based money system. This problem is a worldwide problem and is not isolated to the U.S. economy.

Since 1971, when the United States repudiated the Bretton Woods Agreement that previously allowed central bank holders of U.S. dollars (the world's reserve currency) to redeem dollars for gold, every financial crisis in the world has been a currency crisis. No exceptions.

In the mid-1990s, I spent thirty days in Asia conducting economic briefings to help people in six Asian countries understand what was happening and why it happened. I just returned from Asia, where I conducted another round of briefings on our current impending crisis triggered by the real estate bubble and the subprime mortgage fiasco.

Liquidity Crisis

Unlike ten years ago, this crisis is centered on Wall Street, not in Asia. The resulting economic carnage will be similar but more devastating to more people. More than fifteen years ago, we began warning our readers about the risks surrounding the expansion of the derivatives markets (highly leveraged financial instruments whose value is derived from an underlying security, currency, or commodity). Today's massive growth of debt derivative products is central to the current debt bubble. It is estimated that the notional value of this bubble is six to seven times the world's gross domestic product (GDP). Putting the notional value in terms of dollars, these debt derivatives have grown to over $400 trillion, which is three times as much as all the total domestic debts in the world. Leverage upon leverage upon leverage.

In a world of debt-based money driving a debt-based economy, a false perception of excess liquidity grows a debt bubble of historic proportions. At some point, we reach a tipping point, and lack of real liquidity triggers the bubble to burst. The bursting of the real estate bubble—and more specifically the bursting of the subprime mortgage bubble—hints at what we can expect in the coming months and perhaps years.

Strong Similarities, but More Perilous

Remember the dot-com bubble, where the IPO markets were "blowing and going"? We saw a lot of companies issuing new stock in IPOs (initial public offerings) that was in turn used as "currency" to buy other companies. Kind of like the man who came home one day and explained to his wife that he had sold the family's dog for one hundred thousand dollars. She replied, "You got one hundred thousand dollars for that old dog?" Whereupon the man replied, "Well, sort of. I got two fifty-thousand-dollar cats for the dog." That is well and good as long as the investing public is content to accept "dogs and cats" as money. We all know how the story of the dot-coms and IPOs ended—with a lot of people losing a lot of "money," or asset value.

The current situation is even more onerous, as in addition to current IPOs, many hedge funds were only putting up a small amount of equity in corporate takeover transactions and borrowing the rest. They make this investment attractive by offering perceived diversification by using a new hedging vehicle called "credit default swaps." However, most of these new products are not very liquid. Many of these investment banks were creating funds in-house with other people's money to buy such products. Investment banks are the tip of the iceberg that represents the derivatives bubble that is on a collision course with the "ship" of the world economy.

Bordering on Fraud?

I saw a lead story in a financial publication that touted how the manager of a "successful" hedge fund had just received a $600 million-plus bonus for "good performance." This is where the financial fraud comes in. These derivative products were sold to small hedge funds. Such products are not liquid, and the price of the product is determined largely by the managers of the hedge funds. The hedge funds that own these "exciting new products" just mark up the prices, send the "good news" to their investors, and then write themselves a check as a bonus for "good performance."

This price inflation flows into many other areas. Many of these hedge funds acquired big chunks of stock in smaller companies. Common practice is to price the stock at whatever level they want. Again, the hedge fund managers reward themselves with huge bonuses for "good performance" without ever liquidating the shares. The bubble has its origins in the ability of big name financial institutions to sell hard-to-understand derivative products to investors at inflated prices. The institutions invited these unsuspecting investors to seminars on "wealth building," where most didn't understand a word of what they just heard from the fund managers, other than it was a new and sophisticated, high-tech way to make easy money. The widespread ignorance of these investors was the impetus behind the bubble.

Federal Reserve to the Rescue

The recent action, or inaction, by Fed Chairman Ben Bernanke has been somewhat academic, or "decision by committee." This is far different from what we saw with former Fed Chairman Alan Greenspan when he dealt with the stock market crash of 1987 and other events in between. This leads me to believe that this debacle is so huge that central banks around the world, like the Federal Reserve, have actually lost control over monetary policy. We saw the Federal Reserve add hundreds of billions of dollars of liquidity to the markets, along with lowering the discount rate. The European Central Bank (ECB) put in over $300 billion of liquidity. This is but a drop in the bucket when viewed against the $400 trillion bubble. We know there is a concerted effort to shore up the world economy. These financial markets have been busy creating their own liquidity under the false perception of security in the derivatives market. As reality set in, this credit bubble began to burst, and when these funds that hold derivatives have liquidity problems, they go from "good performance" to default in a New York minute. This credit bubble then burst and dried up liquidity, affecting financial markets everywhere, creating a U.S. recession and eventually a global recession.

When?

This is the big question. The only "glue" holding our debt-based economy and money system together is the reassuring "babble" coming from the mouths of public officials, central bankers, and the Wall Street crowd. Economics is but human action applied against a background of available money, credit, goods, and services in an economic unit. All of the purveyors of "babble" are hard at work reassuring us that "the problem is isolated to a small sector of the economy" and is no big deal. If they are successful, we may delay the "big one" for twenty-four to sixty months. Meanwhile, a terrorist attack, natural disaster, or simply widespread loss of confidence could trigger an economic meltdown in a matter of days or weeks.

What We Know

We can deal all day long in conjecture about when this financial meltdown will occur. However, we know that in just our U.S. economy, which is debt-based and has debt-based money, we pay off debt with newly created debt money (Federal Reserve notes). Our total domestic debt has risen to estimates of between $45–55 trillion. The available currency of exchange to pay the debt or even service the debt (M2) is just a bit over $8 trillion. This means one of two things will happen: (1) default, which will lead to collapse of the entire U.S. economy, or (2) creation of more money and credit to inflate our way out of this current mess (liquidity crisis). Such a remedy is precisely what got us into this mess in the first place.

Economic "Armageddon"?

Many of those attending the private, closed-door meeting in Boston the third week in November 2004 (where press were not allowed) were shocked to hear the dire forecast by Stephen Roach, the chief economist of investment banking giant Morgan Stanley.

An enterprising reporter, Brett Arends of the *Boston Herald*, obtained a copy of Roach's presentation. According to the *Boston Herald* story, Roach's prediction is that America has no better than a 10 percent chance of avoiding economic Armageddon. Roach sees a 30 percent chance of a slump soon and a 60 percent chance "we'll muddle through for a while and delay the eventual Armageddon." The chance we'll get through OK: "one in ten, maybe."

How does Roach come to this dire conclusion? He argues that America's record trade deficit means the dollar will keep falling, and to keep foreigners buying our debt and to prevent skyrocketing inflation, the Federal Reserve will be forced to raise interest rates higher and faster than planned.

Those U.S. consumers who are laden with consumer debt and adjustable rate mortgages will get hammered. Roach apparently used some very alarming facts to support his forecast. Among those cited by the *Boston Herald*:[1]

1. To finance its current account deficit (trade deficit) with the rest of the world, America must import $2.6 billion in cash every working day.

2. The above figure is an amazing 80 percent of the entire world's net savings.

3. This massive borrowing is totally unsustainable.

4. U.S. household debt is at record levels.

5. Twenty years ago, the total debt of U.S. households was equal to half the size of the economy. Today, the figure is 85 percent.

6. Nearly half of new mortgage borrowing is at adjustable interest rates, leaving borrowers much more vulnerable to rate hikes.

7. Americans are already spending a record share of disposable income just to pay interest on debt. And interest rates haven't even risen much yet.

Roach concluded that a "spectacular wave of bankruptcies" is possible.[2]

With our debt-based economy and debt-based monetary system, we have created a debt bubble of record proportions.

There are only two possible scenarios:

1. Massive, widespread default, perhaps even taking down the U.S. banking system

2. Massive creation (printing) of money and credit, and the Federal Reserve deliberately letting the dollar fall and inflation rise, thereby allowing these debtors to pay off their debts with depreciated dollars

Scenario number two is the only option that will prevent a massive collapse of financial institutions. This scenario will, however, cause the collapse of the value of your "loanership" assets such as currency, bank accounts, CDs, bonds, and annuities.

Not pleasant choices, are they? Simply put:

1. Raise interest rates, defend the dollar, and you collapse the economy through massive default and bankruptcies.

2. Let the dollar collapse by creating (printing) more money and credit, and everyone holding paper "loanership" assets gets wiped out in terms of depreciated dollar values of their holdings.

Never lose sight of this one fact: In periods of economic downturn, uncertainty, or outright economic collapse, wealth is not destroyed; it is simply transferred. Money that has value is the transfer agent.

My friends, we find ourselves in a serious economic mess... serious as a heart attack. Economic risk is the least understood and most potentially devastating of all risk.

As Thomas Sowell said in his Townhall.com column, "Poverty and the Left": "Leftists seeking political power show remarkably little interest in the *creation* of wealth, which has raised living standards for the poor, as compared to their obsession with *redistribution*, which has not."[3]

How Will It Affect Me?

If you are prepared, you can be a recipient of huge amounts of wealth transfer. Liquidity will be key. In other words, cash at the crash will be "king." That's cash in your deposit accounts and cash in the form of gold and silver coins. A by-product of such economic malaise will be the human misery surrounding those not prepared.

You must, without delay, warn those you care about and help raise their understanding of how our economy works and how the monetary system works.

The economic storm clouds are on the horizon, and it remains to be seen whether the central bankers can do their "magic" and regain control of monetary policy. My view is they may temporarily delay the big collapse, but the only tool they have to temporarily "fix" the mess is massive money creation. In other words, problems beget solutions that beget bigger problems.

You, my friends, are a select few who understand our situation or have had the opportunity to understand it. The problem may be delayed, but it is not going away.

By Design

Some of you may wonder, "How do you know?" That's simple. I read the writings of the architect of our modern-day economic system. His name is John Maynard Keynes, a British economist. He wrote a book in 1920 titled *The Economic Consequences of the Peace*. In the book, he writes, "By a continuing process of inflation, governments can secretly and unobserved confiscate an important part of the wealth of its citizens. There is no more sure or subtle way to overturn the existing basis of society than to debauch [or destroy] the currency. It engages all the processes of economic law that come down on the side of destruction, and does it in a manner that not one person in a million can diagnose it."[4] Move quickly to get your family's and your financial houses in order. This is no time to be unprepared.

CHAPTER 5

SIMPLE FINANCIAL SOLUTIONS (PART 1)

Living Within Our Means

By Chuck Bates

MUCH HAS BEEN SAID AND WRITTEN WITH REGARD TO the meltdown of the economy over the last few years. My coauthor wrote a prophetic warning almost fifteen years ago in an attempt to prepare folks to get out of the way of the economic tsunami. Additionally there is no lack of blame games going on, from Capitol Hill to Wall Street and back. While a good many politicians and their ill-advised legislation, coupled with greed on Wall Street, account for many of the problems, it was ultimately the consumers—you and me—that share some of the greatest responsibility.

Politicians may have made it too easy to get loans, and banks may have thought up some "creative" financing vehicles, but it was ultimately the consumer who signed on the dotted line. I can hear some of you saying, "We were had. We didn't know they were taking advantage of us!" All I can say to that is, *caveat emptor*: buyers beware.

As we have noted throughout this book, God has given us marvelous gifts, such as discernment and the ability to think before we act. If you do not understand something, then get some advice on the subject. If you don't have a good feeling on a deal, then you probably shouldn't get into it. If you sense that you are one who doesn't have the gift of discernment, then ask God for it in faith, and He will give it to you. Of course, we cannot be experts in all matters of life, but one thing is sure: when you are preparing to sign a contract for a car, a boat, a home mortgage, etc., you had better know what you are getting into, because at that point you cannot feign ignorance. You have already completed the deal, and the wheels are in motion. I cannot deny that there are fraudsters and con artists running around, but we have a responsibility to be wise as serpents, knowing that there is a world out there that often does not have our best interests at heart. This doesn't mean we must go around in fear of our fellow man. We should learn from our experience and the experiences of others who have blazed that trail before us.

We have seen evidence of Congress forcing banks to give loans to people who could not afford them. Banks came up with creative methods of financing these borrowers, and then, knowing these loans would likely be a problem for the bank's balance sheet, they crafted even more creative ways of passing these loans on to others. The hedge fund and portfolio managers were happy to sell these newly created "investments" to folks who wanted bigger and bigger returns on their investments and their retirement accounts. Those would include 401(k) plans and pension plans for teachers, municipal and federal government employees, and union pensions. So you see, a lot of folks got into loans they knew they could not afford, and those holding the loans (mortgages, for the most part) sold them to investors who were looking for unrealistically high returns. In the end, both lost out and began looking for someone to blame for their mistakes.

Keeping Up With the Joneses

Let's face it. All too often we try to keep up with the Joneses, who are trying to keep up with the Smiths, who are trying to keep up with someone else who likely couldn't care less about either the

Joneses or the Smiths. It is an age-old problem. With few exceptions, the economy has been better and life easier for every generation of Americans since World War II. We as parents always want to give our children everything and every advantage, but this has become an obsession for too many of us. The unfortunate side effect has been that some in this new generation lack even a basic understanding of the simplest financial matters or how to prudently manage their money. Some have no basis in reality and are rarely satisfied with what they have; they constantly seek the next thing to do or the latest fad item to purchase. My generation is particularly culpable in this. By and large, we wanted in the first five years of marriage what our parents had after twenty-five to thirty years. With the lowest interest rates since World War II, many of my generation went out and purchased the largest homes they could qualify for. With low interest rates, that amounted to a lot more than they probably would have otherwise undertaken. Many did this, relying on two full-time incomes. And of course, with both partners holding jobs, they had to have two new cars and a two-car garage. Once children arrived, the typical couple found themselves struggling to pay the bills, particularly if one parent ended up staying at home with the children.

Today, there is a very tough economy, with many having taken pay cuts and millions who are simply out of work. The dismal results are announced daily in the newspaper headlines and other media. Foreclosure rates continue to climb, and as long as government constantly intervenes, this trend is likely to continue until the malinvestment is finally liquidated. Bottom line: A great deal of the economic carnage has been brought upon us due to poor stewardship and irresponsibility.

Lust of the Eyes

Let's look at another economic area that has more than its share of people in trouble. The biblical phrase "lust of the eyes" is one of those things everyone struggles with, and many succumb to, especially when it comes to buying things. In America, automobiles are one of those things we think we cannot live without. True, we all need transportation, but do we all need to ride around in the fanciest thing on four wheels? If you cannot truly afford it, then the answer is a resounding NO!

A good friend of mine who passed away a few years back was always astonished at the latest "deals" that were used to get people into new cars. This fellow had been a banker most of his life, having worked as a teller and eventually becoming a bank president. He was absolutely aghast when the major automakers began offering zero interest loans to entice people into buying new cars. He knew what the long-term consequences would be for both the borrower and the lender: economic catastrophe. The borrowers became slaves to the notes they had signed, and the lenders (the financing arm of the auto companies) found themselves stuck with loans that produced little and had a huge default rate. The increasingly long terms of the loans resulted in people still paying on auto loans at the point when they needed to trade for another car. Essentially they were "under water" because they were still paying for the first car, but the loan balance exceeded the market value of the car. The balance on the first loan had to be tacked onto the new car loan, which meant the individual was truly a slave to the car note.

Eventually, automakers had a hard time justifying the loans and special "deals" they had offered. With the tightening of credit, the auto sector had to face the fact that they had been financing cars for people who, in a normal economic environment, would likely not have qualified for loans in the first place.

Unfortunately, Americans have grown so accustomed to this ritual of car "ownership" that they expect the dealers to get us whatever we want—at a low cost and with minimal credit. But again, with tightening in the credit markets, the car companies found themselves in a quandary: they couldn't sell cars unless they financed them for the customer—but the low credit scores resulting from too much debt has made that nearly impossible.

Even with the Cash for Clunkers government program, the overall auto sector continues to suffer. As a matter of fact, individual creditworthiness in the United States has become so bad that immediately after the Cash for Clunkers deal was over, a local Toyota dealership owner in my area told me how he had to repossess over 40 percent of the cars they had sold under the program. Within just two months, these car buyers were already behind on the notes, and the cars were coming back to the dealerships due to bad and worsening credit among consumers. Keep in mind that while Toyota makes some pretty good cars, these are not Mercedes-Benz these people were buying. These were small to midsize cars, typically selling for less than the national average of twenty thousand dollars for a new car. I confirmed this with other dealers in the area, and they recounted exactly the same experience.

Friends, our nation and specifically much of my generation have lived well outside our means. New cars, newer and bigger homes, bigger televisions, and fancy vacations once or twice a year to ever-more exotic and pricey locales has all added up to incredible debt and dysfunction for families across the nation. One-third of the families of four currently carries month-to-month debt of over $15,000 in credit card debt alone![1] Additionally, we should note that many of these families make less than $50,000 per year.[2] Using the median interest rates charged by credit card companies, that equates to over $2,700 per year—*just in interest payments!* This is roughly equal to $225 per month per household just to service the debt, and this debt is growing. While we did see a reduction in the national average in early 2009, due to the abrupt wake-up call regarding the economy in the fall of 2008, credit card offers are still coming in the mail, and Americans are still eager to use them.[3] Let's face it; they are easy to use—too easy. Bankruptcy rates are again hitting all-time highs; the incredible pressure this is putting on the American family is resulting in rising divorce rates as well. We discuss the results of this in another chapter, but suffice it to say it only begets new problems—that require new solutions—that the government is happy to meddle in. And the church, which should be a source of prudent counsel for believers, is a little behind the curve in dealing with these problems.

I want to be absolutely clear: I am not suggesting we all live in shacks, wear potato sacks, and ride bicycles to work. I do believe God does want us to prosper; He has given us the means to do so if we will use some wisdom and stewardship to that end. I do not ascribe to a poverty mentality, but I do believe we should live in reality. If you make $30,000 per year, you should not even think about purchasing a $200,000+ home, or for that matter a $130,000 home. You cannot afford it. That is not an attempt to diminish your faith in God's provision or to keep you down; it is simple math.

The Bible tells us our God owns the cattle on a thousand hills. Obviously, prosperity is a gift from God, available to us as His children. Scripture tells us that if we are faithful in little, He will make us faithful in more; however, we must appropriate His wisdom in all matters, and this certainly includes our finances. In Proverbs we are admonished to pay attention to the ant and its work ethic. The ant has its God-given instinct to get out of the weather and prepare its home. Throughout the animal kingdom, we see that all animals prepare for the change in seasons. You may be thinking, "But Chuck, you are talking about animals, and they don't have mortgages and college loans to pay!" That's true; they don't have need of such things. But even the ant takes care of the basics and is not waiting on the Lord to do a miracle for it. How much more responsibility do we, as God's creations, have for appropriating His wisdom and counsel?

Scripture is clear that the borrower is servant to the lender, and while it is not a sin to borrow money for a home or an important project, we have to be smart about how we go about it. We are admonished to consider the costs before going into something, and we need to think before we leap in matters of finance. Don't let that be an excuse not to act when you know you should, but keep in mind that the best decisions are made when good sense prevails over emotion. There is a reason retail stores have grab items in the checkout line; we are all too willing to succumb to impulse and buy them. It is no different when it comes to pricier items. Homes and automobiles can be emotion-driven commitments, and we need to exercise the good sense God has given us, so as not to fall into the trap of unnecessary indebtedness. If we are honest, we will admit that none of us like to be in debt. When you make a final payment on a big item, you feel absolutely liberated from the weight of the commitment.

You may have been in such debt for so long that you have forgotten what life was like without it. But let me tell you, there is a better way. Have I ever taken on debt for a big item? Yes, I have, but never more than I knew that I could pay over a reasonable period of time. I also believe it is important to have a certain amount of savings to cushion your finances in the event you lose a job or have an unexpected event in your life.

You see, too many Americans are running their economic engines with the throttle to the floor all the time. None of us would drive our cars that way, but we are all too willing to drive our check-books and credit cards in such a manner. Eventually you burn up the engine, or in this case, your finances. You end up in ruin if you continue down that path. Let me give you a perfect example.

A previous employee called to say he was considering investing some money he "had come into." Eventually, he did not invest the money but instead bought some things for his house, then went on an expensive vacation. I learned that the money he had "come into" was a home equity line he had taken out on a house he had purchased with practically nothing down. I hope he and his wife took a lot of pictures on the trip because it was likely the last one for a while.

This is insanity, friends, but bad decision making is not relegated only to the young. A few years ago I had an opportunity to work with clients who had built up a business; however, due to some circumstances outside of their control, along with some really bad business decisions, this couple found themselves with over $2 million in assets but nearly $4 million in debt—and no real way to get out of it.

Simple Solutions

The examples are too numerous to put in twenty volumes of books, but the solution is simple: we must live within and—if possible—*beneath* our means. Again, I am not suggesting you live in squalor.

Smart homebuying

If you are a young couple looking at your first home purchase, look at something that is within two-thirds to three quarters of what you "qualify" for. For instance, if you qualify for a home valued at $150,000, look for homes in the $100,000 to $115,000 area. This will still likely get you a nice home—perhaps a foreclosure situation or a house that needs a little work—and will still leave some cushion in the monthly budget so that you are not a slave to the house payment. Now take my advice and don't use the savings for a new car; put it in savings, because life will deliver some surprises. Those reading this book with a few years of wisdom under your belt know exactly what I am writing is the absolute truth. That new house is going to know when you have some extra money—a roof repair or the need for a new water heater will invariably crop up to "eat" your extra cash.

Eventually, children may be in the picture—or perhaps a child you did not expect—and there will be the costs associated with that. The birth of a child should be a joyous event, but if you are a slave to debt, it may seem like an additional burden. This shouldn't be so.

If your family income does not allow you to comfortably purchase a home, then you should continue to rent until you have saved enough money to make such a move. Again, make up your minds to look at homes below your means. This will make for a much happier marriage and family. Keep in mind that you are "renting" one way or the other, as you are paying rent to the land-lord or the banker every month. The exception, of course, is if you are fortunate enough to buy the house with cash. The advantage with renting is that you don't have any long-term responsibilities for the property.

As you can see, all of this really does come down to common sense. Unfortunately, in the years leading up to the real estate bubble and the subsequent crash, many Americans have been willing to throw caution—and good sense—to the wind. The results have been devastating for many.

Another option is purchasing a home that is in the process of foreclosure. You may be tempted to accuse me of practicing "vulture" economics, where you make out with a good deal while your neighbor's bones are being picked. Nothing could be further from the truth. One man's foreclosure is another's discount dream home. It is true that the fellow purchasing the foreclosure is likely getting a great deal, but in about half of the states in the nation, the buyer of the foreclosure is doing a great service to the one who lost the home. You see, in those twenty to twenty-five states that do *not* allow the borrower to simply walk away from their respon-sibility to pay the mortgage, the borrower is still on the hook for any amount still owed above the selling price of the home. Let's say that someone falls on hard times and they owe $200,000 on the home and the home sells in foreclosure for $150,000. The orig-inal owner still owes the $50,000 difference. The new buyer can help the previous owner by reducing the debtor's balance by the $150,000 purchase price. Often the bank is then willing to nego-tiate on the remainder of the debt.

Alternatively, if the person facing foreclosure lives in one of the states that lets homeowners walk away from a home they can no longer afford, it will still have long-term ramifications on their credit and their ability to purchase a home in the future; so purchasing a foreclosed home may help not only your wallet but also the person who needs relief from their burdensome home.

Frugal vacationing

If you need a vacation, consider your own state rather than an expensive trip to the other side of the globe. Perhaps consider taking your family on a short-term mission trip with your church. The cost will likely be less, and you will gain an invaluable family experience. Live below your means, but do so without a spirit of poverty. Don't be cheap—but don't be unwise either. Purchase quality when shopping for real needs and you will likely save in the long run. Just make sure it is quality and not just a hyped-up name or fad. Think "long term" in all of your financial decisions.

We can all prosper within our means. Whether you make a household income of $30,000 or $1 million, we all are called to be good stewards of it. It all belongs to the Lord anyway, and therefore we have a great responsibility to use it wisely. Keep this in mind when you are considering a purchase or making a decision on how to best protect your funds from the ups and downs of the market and the volatility of the dollar. Money answers all things, and we need to use it for the benefit of the kingdom. God gives us the resources, and He is more than willing to give us guidance on how to use it, multiply it, and use it again.

CHAPTER 6

SIMPLE FINANCIAL SOLUTIONS (PART 2)

Real Prescriptions for the Health Care Problem

By Chuck Bates

W E ALL WANT TO FEEL GOOD. NO ONE REALLY WANTS to be sick. From health food to health clubs and from insurance to Medicare almost all Americans are looking for ways to remain healthy, or at least for a method to care for whatever ails them. The health care debate is nothing new in this country, and long before Barack Obama made the scene and began his push for nationalized health programs there were the likes of FDR, LBJ, and even Bill Clinton, via his wife, attempting to change the ways Americans receive health care. So what are the real problems with the system, and is it repairable? Should we look at other nations as a role model, and if not, then what are the solutions to this debate that has taken center stage for the last few years? Let's get to the real prescription to America's health care debate.

Much of what President Obama and the Democrats in Congress center their argument on is the "inefficiency" and "unfairness" supposedly inherent to the nation's health care industry. They attribute much of the blame to greed on the part of insurance companies, pharmaceutical companies, doctors, and hospitals, but never do they look at what really has driven the majority of health care costs over the last half of a century—government regulation.

Sure, the big pharmaceutical companies have made increasingly greater profits as the nation as a whole has moved toward solving health problems with a little pill. Some of the advancements in pharmacology have indeed saved lives or at the very least prolonged them. The companies with the best products should reap the rewards of their labor, but the increasing costs of overregulation are a large part of the costs attributable in the creation of new drugs.

Doctors, as a whole, usually do well financially, but most of us don't consider the costs associated with a doctor's work. Physicians face higher costs for malpractice insurance due to the jackpot justice doled out by juries swayed by slick trial lawyers. They also face higher costs in their clinics due to new government regulation year after year. Additionally, many physicians are feeling a financial pinch when they serve Medicare or Medicaid patients, as they might receive 20 percent of normal fees and at times actually lose money treating one of these patients who on average are twenty times more likely to sue the physician! Talk about playing Russian roulette.

Insurance companies seem to be taking the brunt of the administration's and the Left's scorn, where the media has been used as a casting director to mold public opinion in what seems to be an unrelenting barrage of bad press and outright falsehoods aimed at villainizing the entire industry as a bunch of heartless, greedy, corporate monopoly men. While there is *some* truth to the way *some* insurance companies have treated *some* policyholders, the vast majority of companies are simply reacting to market forces that require them to raise rates. Ultimately, if you have insurance, you are a part of the insurance company too. You have simply taken out a policy that makes you part of a pool of dollars that is nothing more than a collective assumption of risk. You are partaking in a sort of co-op in hopes you never need to use the products. Are you a greedy, money-hungry, corporate monopoly man? I didn't think so.

Of course we don't want to leave out the hospitals. The Left has accused the hospitals of taking advantage of the patients, but in reality we must realize that hospitals are businesses. That's right;

a hospital is a business, and whether it is a nonprofit or for-profit enterprise, it must balance the books just like any other business if it intends to continue its service to the community.

This business reality in health care is unfortunately something too many Americans have never given a moment's thought to. Americans in general have become so accustomed to immediate service when it comes to their health care that they don't stop to think that there are costs associated with that care. Fewer yet realize just how much of that cost is attributable to government overregulation. Who can blame them, as there are many in government and elsewhere who have literally proclaimed health care as some sort of constitutional right? Let me be clear that it is NOT a right but indeed a responsibility. As we discuss in other chapters, the founders of this great land believed, and rightfully so, that we all have certain unalienable rights from God, among them life, liberty, and the pursuit of happiness. Now, while I believe we serve the Great Physician, almighty God, I also visit a doctor now and then for a remedy to aid this fleshly body I live in. I do not expect someone else to pick up the tab. I plan for such contingencies by purchasing health insurance for my family. It is all part of my responsibility to care and provide for my family.

Health Care Entitlement

Where did this entitlement to health care or health insurance come from? Well, you may not like the answer, but again, we can look to government interference and regulation as a big starting point. During World War II the federal government enacted wage controls in an effort to manage industries and their payrolls so that companies could not offer better pay and easily lure employees away from one industry to another. As a result, the companies had to think of alternatives to sweeten the pot, so to speak, and health insurance benefits became one of those sweeteners. It may shock you to know

58

that health insurance at that time was by far the exception rather than the rule. Ordinarily one would only go to a doctor if they had an absolute need and paid for the services rendered and hoped it would be a long time before they had to make another visit to see the physician or the physician had to come to see them. (Strange to think of a doctor making a house call, but it used to be a regular practice.) The same was true for hospital stays, few and far between. Now clearly there have been enormous advances in medicine, but the rise in health care costs have far outpaced all of these medical advances, and again there is one common denominator: government regulation and intervention in the system.

For those who think I am overly critical of the role government has played in our current health care debacle, allow me to offer some irrefutable evidence. My father-in-law, George Trent, is a past president of Methodist Hospitals of Tennessee. He spent his career in hospital and health care administration. He built Healthcare Corporation of America's first hospital, was administrator of Vanderbilt University's School of Medicine, and eventually ran the Methodist system of nearly thirty hospitals at one time. He is also a past president of the Tennessee Hospital Association and a Life Fellow of the American College of Health Care Executives.

I note all of this to simply demonstrate that he knows a thing or two about health care. In 1965 his cost per patient per day was about $9.50. Just eighteen months later that figure had soared to almost $70 per day! What accounted for such a dramatic rise in the cost of health care, you ask? Medicare and Medicaid were signed into law. That's right; in less than two years, the costs to hospitals to care for patients went up over 700 percent! Within four years of the creation of Medicare and Medicaid, his costs per patient per day had skyrocketed to well over $370 per day. It is important to note that this was the cost to the hospital, not the profit. When I asked George the reasons, he said the additional red tape and bureaucracy created by these huge government programs added such a burden as to require additional staff and steps to carry out the same care they were providing patients before the programs were created.

Welcome to government-run health care. As I noted, the push by government for the control of our health care systems has been waging for some time now, and Barack Obama is just the latest spokesman for the socializing of medicine in the United States.

In an interview with Richard L. Scott, the founder of Columbia Hospital Corporation, which eventually merged to form Columbia/ HCA, the largest hospital company in the world, he described the extreme dangers of additional interference by government in the field of health care and noted, "More government rules always drive costs up, and it always hurts the poorest people."[1] However he also offered some basic, common-sense, free-market solutions to the problem facing our health care system and costs.

> In every industry in this country there is waste. So the only thing that has worked in any industry is to get the individual that is going to use the service to be more financially accountable for making the decisions. That is the only way we can do it. So we need to give you the same tax breaks that employers get so you buy your own insurance. It's your insurance policy, like your own car insurance policy, and you know that if you drive too fast it is going to cost you more. You really think more about how you stay healthy, eat right, exercise....Let you buy the policy you want....We need to allow insurance companies to sell across state lines. So if one state has a whole bunch of mandates that cause their insurance to go up if you live in that state, you can buy insurance from the next state, which doesn't have as many mandates. There is clearly waste in the system, but it is the individual that is going to ferret it out.

Mr. Scott went further to compare auto coverage to health insurance, stating, "Think about auto insurance. You don't buy insurance for things you know you have to spend on that year. Maybe you know that you are going to have to have new tires; you don't get insurance to buy these new tires. In health care we say we want insurance to cover minor things such as a doctor's office visit even though we know we are going to have a couple of these a year." Mr. Scott makes a very good point in emphasizing common sense and personal responsibility for necessary health maintenance. We have become a society of health care entitlement brats. We want to cast off basic responsibility and pretend that someone else is picking up the tab. This has lead to a huge waste of services and in turn has driven a lot of the additional costs in our health system.

There are a couple of examples of true free-market principles playing out in today's health care market: laser eye surgery and cosmetic surgery. Both are typically not covered by insurance providers and are deemed elective in nature. As such there is no insurance subsidy, and those who would seek to have laser eye treatment to correct their vision or those who would seek to enhance their physical appearance through cosmetic surgery must do so out of their own pockets.

When it is coming directly out of our pockets, people are very apt to shop around for a good price as well as a good doctor, and this competition has actually resulted in lower prices in these two fields. Ultimately this is good for the consumer as well as the doctor as he or she increases the volume of their business and the customer gets a competitive rate. Noting these examples, why not set aside money for doctor visits we know we are going to likely have to make each year and shop around for the best doctors at the best prices? Mr. Scott noted, "Think; you will figure a better price than a third-party insurance company and think about the costs of the checks and balances where they have to go and send a bill to a third party to see if it was done right. All it does is increase the costs of health care."

He is right. Not too long ago our little girl, like so many, decided to put something in her ear that did not belong there. We took her to the nearest minor-care facility to remove the foreign object. The clerk at the counter informed me that if I paid out of pocket that evening, I would receive a 60 percent discount on whatever service was necessary to take care of our daughter. It sounded good to me (although I would have spared no expense for our daughter's health), and what would have cost over one hundred fifty dollars ended up costing sixty-two dollars. Why? Simply because I had cut out the middleman and the urgent-care facility had received their payment without the hassle and the paperwork of a third-party insurance carrier. Clean and easy, and our daughter received top-notch care while learning a valuable lesson not to ever put things in her ears again. One for the scrapbooks I suppose. We left the facility with clean ears and an only slightly lighter wallet.

Conversely, a facility that is attempting to receive payment from a third-party insurance company or worse yet the government via Medicare or Medicaid is most assuredly going to bill at much higher rates to compensate for the additional paperwork, delay in payment, and the reduction in final rate by the government programs. As noted, most physicians and hospitals receive only a fraction of their regular fee when treating Medicare and Medicaid patients. The government has essentially dictated to the doctors what their work is worth. I have spoken to many doctors who are indeed losing money when they serve these patients, and a number of them have stopped taking patients who are using the Medicare or Medicaid programs. I asked Mr. Scott about the impact on hospitals as well, and he stated:

> You get paid dramatically less than you get paid from the insurance industry, and so you are typically charging anybody who is buying insurance more than what Medicare is paying and for sure what Medicaid is paying you. So there is clearly a shifting of costs to the private sector. It goes on all the time. At the same time there are many more rules for Medicare and Medicaid that cause the cost to go up. Who gets hurt the most is the individual walking into

the emergency room with no insurance because then the
rates are way more expensive.

This is evidence of government intervention with unreasonable
reimbursements to the health care industry while adding additional
rules that have forced both doctors and hospitals to shift the costs
to those of us with insurance and the rest of the private sector, thus
raising our insurance rates year after year. There truly is no such
thing as a free lunch, as someone has to pay the costs. Mr. Scott
again noted the difference between health insurance and other types
of insurance, saying, "Why don't we have the same problems with
auto insurance? The reason we don't is that you own the policy. You
don't have the same sort of government regulations covering everything. You know that your actions have an impact on the cost of
your insurance, so you have a real accountable industry. In health
care we don't do that."

Again the point is made that the individual has a responsibility
not only to provide for his own health care but also to spend those
health care dollars wisely. Let's look at some of the free-market
solutions to the current crisis.

HSAs: A Suitable Alternative

In the last year we decided to take our companies to a Health
Savings Account plan (HSA). In case you are unfamiliar with
HSAs, they are essentially insurance plans that allow the individual or employee to deposit funds throughout the year into an
interest-bearing savings account tax free. If a health need arises, the
individual can use a debit card to pay for that need directly from
the HSA. In addition, these types of plans also have what is often
referred to as a "catastrophic care" policy attached to them. Simply
the individual is responsible for his or her health costs up to say
$2,500 to $5,000, and if something major should occur, the health

insurance policy kicks in to take care of the really big expenses. We decided to move to this type of plan for several reasons:

1. It lowered the monthly premiums for almost all of our employees.

2. It allows the employee many more options on how and where to spend their health care dollars than a traditional health insurance plan. For example, most policies don't cover eye glasses or chiropractic, but under an HSA the participant can apply their savings account dollars to virtually anything health related.

3. It promotes responsibility of the individual to think before they use their insurance.

4. Should the employee leave, they can take the HSA with them as it is completely portable. No more worrying about insurance coverage between jobs.

Let's focus on the responsibility that comes with an HSA. Over the years I have had employees who went to the doctor seemingly just because they had insurance to pay for it. I recall one in particular who was constantly going to the doctor for some odd reason or another. It was as though she enjoyed spending insurance money just because it was there. The end result is that the additional use added to the burden of the insurance company and was one of the reasons we saw increased premiums almost yearly. This employee had no reason to be responsible in her medical spending because it cost her little to nothing personally.

On another occasion, a young employee demonstrated little wisdom by going to an emergency room for a sore throat one weekend instead of waiting until Monday to go and see her regular physician. What would have amounted to a $25 co-pay at the time turned into a $2,500 ER visit that was not covered and ended up costing the employee personally, as it was not a regular visit and her deductible was almost equal to the cost of the hospital visit. Tough lesson, but I rather doubt she will make that mistake twice. This was a sore throat, not a broken arm or a cardiac arrest!

People just don't seem to think when it comes to spending health care dollars, especially if they are not used to it costing them anything personally. An HSA requires the individual to think before they act. If it is a little sniffle, they can use the account to purchase cold medicine, and if that doesn't work, they can use it to pay for a doctor's visit and the prescription the doctor prescribes. It gives the individual the choices and the responsibility for their health care.

Finding Affordable Health Care Coverage Across State Lines

Many have noted the need for additional freedom to purchase insurance coverage across state lines. What is unbelievable to me is that I can go online and purchase an automobile or even a firearm from across the other side of the country, but I cannot purchase health insurance outside of the state of my principle residence!

The result for many is that their home state may have ridiculous mandates, forcing insurance companies to cover almost every possible ailment (real or perceived). The state forces these companies to raise rates to pay for all of the treatments, while a neighboring state may not have so many mandates, making insurance more affordable for its citizens. So the fellow in the high-rate state has to take what is dished out to him without the opportunity to shop across state lines for a better rate. Let's look at an example.

In Massachusetts, state regulators are yielding to pressure from lobbyists representing certain "fringe" medical groups (psychiatrists, counselors, specialists) to cover all sorts of ailments that would not ordinarily be covered. Compare that to a state such as Kansas that requires more basic health coverage mandates and you immediately note a lower cost for coverage. According to ehealthinsurance.com, a family in Kansas City can likely purchase comprehensive coverage for less than $200 per month, while a family in Boston will likely pay more than $760 for similar coverage.

Back to the auto insurance analogy. I can pick and choose my coverage, my deductibles, etc., but with the typical health policy I have much less say in what I am paying for and even less in where I can go and spend my health care dollars.

The Real Numbers Behind America's Uninsured

Having looked at various issues facing health insurance coverage, let's take a brief look at a very misleading statement made by the president as well as many others pushing for nationalized health care. The White House constantly declares that over 47 million Americans are without health insurance. This number is completely erroneous. First, it includes approximately 12 to 15 million illegal immigrants. Once we subtract those from the total, we are now at 32 to 35 million. Now subtract approximately another 15 million who are in between eighteen and thirty-five years of age and think of themselves as bulletproof and without need for regular coverage, and that figure drops to, say, 17 to 20 million. Now we have to subtract all of the uninsured children less than eighteen years of age, as they are already covered by the State Children's Health Insurance Program (SCHIP) mandated in every state. Once it is all said and done and we subtract even those who are just too lazy to sign up for Medicaid, we are left with an estimated number of 3 to 6 million Americans who simply cannot qualify or cannot afford basic health insurance due to either their financial situation or a preexisting condition.

Now, I don't know about you, but if the current system is working fairly well for the vast majority of those using it, I don't think it is a good idea to turn the entire system on its ear to take care of 2 percent of the population. If we need to develop some sort of safety net or better aid charity hospitals and clinics to care for these folks, then by all means let's work to that end, but common sense would dictate you don't kick everyone off the freeway and force them to buy a government car because one person has a flat tire!

Based on the figures above and comments from those who are in the health care field, one has to ask why the president and his adherents want to take over health care. Simply put, it boils down to control. How can I be so certain? Well, socialized medicine has been an utter failure everywhere it has been tried. Just look at Great Britain or Canada as examples.

In Canada you can wait nearly two years just to see a doctor about a heart problem. Last year one Canadian province ran out of funds and had to put off six thousand surgeries until the next fiscal year! In Britain the government is offering lucrative deals to eye surgeons in the United States to spend three to six months in the United Kingdom to do basic cataract surgery, as they don't have enough specialists to cover even this basic procedure.

Government control destroyed incentive, which led to a shortage of new doctors. In addition, it added a huge burden, as it was touted as "free health care," which gave the people no incentive to be judicious in their use of the system, which also created shortages. Seeing that it fails everywhere it is tried, it can lead us to one and only one conclusion: socialists want to control us at every turn, and what better way to control your population than to control their health care.

Furthering this premise is the absolute avoidance by the Obama administration of the free-market alternatives we have outlined in this chapter. Republicans have forwarded at least five health care proposals that have received scant attention by the media and even less from the president and congressional leaders.

Medical Liability Reform

One final aspect to health care that would immediately bring down costs but the powers that be are unwilling to consider is the necessity of medical tort liability reform. You can hardly turn on your television these days without seeing a trial lawyer or ambulance chaser running an advertisement to perceived "victims" of medicine and pharmaceutical companies, talking about the money they can get if they will just sue somebody.

We know for a fact that almost every doctor in America is being forced to practice defensive medicine, ordering tests that they know are likely to yield little result but do so out of concern of being sued by some opportunist attorney. A surgeon friend of mine effectively ran 9.9 out of 10 tests on a patient prior to a surgery. The patient was terribly obese and failed to tell the doctor of some of his condition. Despite the warnings of the surgeon, the patient elected to go ahead with the surgery and shortly thereafter died due to a complication that was not directly associated with the procedure. Despite the surgeon doing more than his due diligence, the family of the patient sued the doctor three separate times. Each time he was exonerated of any wrongdoing but at the cost of nearly one million dollars. As a result his malpractice insurance rates went up, he refused to work on obese patients again, and he eventually got out of medicine and went into early retirement from active medical practice, leaving a gaping whole to be filled in his local hospital.

In Mississippi, trial lawyers were getting such whopping jackpot justice judgments against physicians that it raised malpractice rates so high virtually every OB/GYN physician was leaving the state! Thankfully the state legislature and Governor Haley Barbour passed and signed into law some medical tort liability reform in the form of caps on judgments, and the result was a return of specialists to the state as the malpractice rates began to drop.

The Obama-Pelosi-Reid health care bill actually penalizes states that seek to rein in some of these out-of-control trial lawyers and dangles a carrot in the form of billions of dollars to states that don't mess with the trial lawyer racket. Why, you ask? Simple, the trial lawyers are some of the biggest political donors to the Democratic Party. They, along with the abortion industry and unions, are the virtual ATM machine for Democratic candidates. That is why the Obama bill mandates tax dollars be spent on abortion, as well as mandates parts of health care be forced to unionize. Can you imagine your nurse, or worse yet your doctor, telling you in the emergency room you will have to wait until their union break is over? How about a government health care bureaucrat getting in the middle between you and your doctor as you attempt to make decisions vital to your health or your children's health?

Friends, there are simple solutions to the costs of health care in our country, and as we have discussed, it begins with us and the freedom to make commonsense choices and to use fiscal restraint. Personal responsibility is the first priority, and an understanding that health care is not a right. Secondly, we need to allow the free market to do what it does best, and that will lead to more competition that is healthy for the economy and the individual as it lowers costs and leads to innovation. Finally, we must reduce the size and scope of government, as it is seeking to completely control one-sixth of the economy via the takeover of health care.

A little known fact in the president's health proposal is the IRS will be handling the management of the program with real-time access to all of your financial data. Friends, that is scary business! We used to joke that a national health scare scheme would have the efficiency of the post office and the compassion of the IRS. Little did we know just how close to a reality that would become.

It is up to us to fight for our right of freedom of choice when it comes to our health care needs. You can find additional information on the costs of nationalized health care across the Web, but a few sites to consider would include www.heritage.org and www.docs4patientcare.org. Information is vital, and action without information is fanaticism, so do your homework and get involved now or someone from the government will be making your health care decisions for you.

CHAPTER 7

SIMPLE FINANCIAL SOLUTIONS (PART 3)

Get to Work; No Free Lunches Here

By Chuck Bates

THE WORD OF GOD IS VERY CLEAR ON THE MATTER OF work. Work is mentioned nearly eight hundred times throughout Scripture. We are familiar with the passage, "If any would not work, neither should he eat" (2 Thess. 3:10, KJV). There are verses that deal with a laborer's work, a master's work, working with your employees, contract labor, full-time labor, and skilled craftsmen and tradesmen. There are also verses pertaining to the fate of those who are too lazy to work. We are commanded to do the work of the Lord, to work in our communities, to be active in the work of the leadership of those communities, to work for the benefit of widows and orphans, and to work in the church. Why is it, then, that so many inside the institution that calls itself the church—as well as society in general—have such an aversion to something so basic? Simply put, work equals pain.

Since we got booted out of the Garden of Eden, man has had to go to work. Sure, we can blame Adam and Eve for the expulsion or for their sin nature, but that won't put food on the table. God said to Adam in Genesis 3:17–19, "Because you have heeded the voice of your wife, and have eaten from the tree of which I commanded you, saying, 'You shall not eat of it': Cursed is the ground for your sake; in toil you shall eat of it all the days of your life. Both thorns and thistles it shall bring forth for you, and you shall eat the herb of the field. In the sweat of your face you shall eat bread till you return to the ground."

Clearly, the free lunch was over. From that point on, we would have to work to feed and clothe ourselves daily. Again, work is pain, and since that time we have seen throughout history how man constantly devises schemes to live off the labor of others so that he can avoid pain. Whether it be the street thug who steals rather than work, the corporate wimp who attempts to legislate himself a living instead of working for it in the marketplace, the lazy bum who would rather live on welfare than get a job, or the pastor who strips his congregation of their hard-earned money while he lives in a mansion and they struggle to pay rent—people are always trying to get out of working. Real work is hard, but it need not be something we try to avoid. There are parts of my work that I care less for than others, but overall I enjoy my work and the fruit of my labors.

Sadly, there are others who constantly try to live off my labors and yours rather than going to work themselves. Politics is one of the most glaring examples. The whole career of many politicians consists of working to get elected so they can work to pass legislation that takes our money, which will be spent to benefit their constituents, who in turn vote to keep the politicians in office.

We all recognize how wrong it is to live off of the labor of others when we are capable of working but refuse to do so. Many churches today are preaching a pseudo gospel of wealth and prosperity that conveys the fraudulent idea that by simply giving all they have to this ministry or that, they will suddenly hit the heavenly lottery and all their problems will be solved. Others give with the anticipation that God is some sort of slot machine that pays off if you put enough dollars in the offering plate. Still others are preaching that by "faith" you can simply run around a Cadillac or Mercedes seven times and it will miraculously be yours. These kinds of "faith" practices will only leave you frustrated and dizzy. The Cadillac or Mercedes dealer will be happy to sell you a car, but the "luxury sedan rain dance" will not likely result in your driving away with the vehicle.

But we cannot survive these turbulent times living off of someone else's work. We have to do our part so that we can receive the true blessings of God that have no sorrow attached to them.

I believe we serve a God who, in the words of Scripture, "owns the cattle on a thousand hills." (See Psalm 50:10.) He is willing to add to us and make us responsible for as much as we are proven trustworthy to handle for His glory. I also believe that God will meet our every need and will often do so above and beyond what we anticipate—and in ways we may not expect. Unfortunately, entire "ministries" have been based on a "health and wealth" gospel that is not too far removed from the emotional pep speeches of Tony Robbins. They have little to do with the God of the Bible and everything to do with feeding the corporate machine that masquerades as their "ministry." Ultimately they leave a great deal of carnage in their paths because those who have trusted in the "health and wealth" gospel have failed to listen to God. Instead, they have allowed themselves to be manipulated emotionally to give all they had, while failing to take care of their own financial responsibilities.

I have seen God move in my own life when I have been obedient to give in faith, beyond what my rational mind would probably allow. However, I do not believe He would tell me to cast all fiduciary responsibility to the wind and not feed and house my family first. Scripture notes that a man who does not care for his family has denied the faith and is worse than a heathen. Further, Scripture declares that a man should first prepare his land and then build his house. It also admonishes us to consider the cost before we begin to build (1 Tim. 5:8; Prov. 24:27; Luke 14:28–32). These are basic principles for life that, if applied, help us avoid a lot of pitfalls.

The Bible also advises us that riches gained quickly are *rarely long lived*—that hard work is *honorable*—and theft and laziness are to be *condemned*. When politicians or preachers tell you that you can get some material thing for nothing, they are lying. Someone had to work for it first. In many of the churches that preach the wealth and prosperity gospel, the pastor may be globe-trotting in one or more private jets, riding to the church in a limousine, and living in a mansion. At the same time, many in the congregation are barely making ends meet but giving almost all they have to support the pastor's lifestyle. The preacher may appear to be a living, breathing example of the prosperity gospel he preaches, but the prosperity of his eternal soul may be in serious jeopardy.

Again don't misunderstand me. I do believe that God wants His children to prosper, but not everyone is going to ride around in a Rolls-Royce or live in a palace like some Saudi sheikh. For the pastors reading this book, let me be clear that I do not believe a pastor is more humble or closer to God when the congregation keeps him poor. I believe—and the Bible backs this up—that a worker is worthy of his hire. At the same time, I see in my own community as well as across the nation and around the globe those preachers who are fleecing the sheep instead of feeding them. We are warned of this in Ezekiel chapter 34. We also know that money is necessary for the furthering of the gospel and to help meet the needs of those who are truly in need due to circumstances beyond their control. Scripture specifically mentions widows and orphans. Clearly, money is a tool to be used for building up the kingdom of Christ, but at the same time, the love of it is the root of many kinds of evil.

Do you go to church anticipating the outpouring of the Holy Spirit in your life—for the impartation of the Word in a sermon—and to celebrate what He has accomplished for the kingdom through you during the week? Or do you go expecting a financial windfall? Be honest with yourself. It is true that we cannot outgive God, but what is our motive for giving and fellowshiping with the body of believers?

The Fleecing of the Congregation

Several years ago a client invited me to visit his church and I accepted. The first week I was taken aback by what appeared to be questionable doctrine, but I gave it a second chance and came back the following week. The second visit was my last visit to this particular church. I saw a lot of well-meaning folks who undoubtedly wanted to be there to celebrate the Lord and to know more about Him. However, the doctrine that was being foisted on the people was overtly "wealth and prosperity" driven. It was sickening. I saw families who were likely just barely paying their bills, being pushed to give all they had for the "pastor's appreciation offering." What's more, my client came running up to me in a frenzy, excited that someone in the congregation had just given the pastor a brand-new Mercedes-Benz sedan! Immediately, an elder in the church rose to the podium and declared that the congregation needed to dig deep and give to the pastor's offering. He reminded the congregation that they had recently given a well-known televangelist $35,000 the night he spoke—and they needed to do more for their own pastor that morning.

Now, some of you are picking your jaw up off the floor while others may be asking what's wrong with blessing your pastor financially. Nothing is wrong with it, but the manipulations being used to separate those folks from the content of their wallets was disgusting. Further, this was a church where the pastor was already paid a handsome sum—close to one million dollars per year! Now, I would submit that he was already overappreciated—and if he wanted a Mercedes-Benz, he could have gone to the local dealership and purchased one very easily. I am not belittling the givers, but I have to wonder about their motives, as well as the motives of the preacher and his staff. Lately, this same church has fallen on hard times, as have a number of such prosperity gospel–driven congregations. Instead of seeking God's wisdom and provision, they had relied solely on emotion as a tool to motivate giving. As a result, they drained the congregation dry financially. Consequently, the members were not prepared for the economic drought the country is experiencing now. The building is now for sale, and another church congregation is likely to purchase it in the coming months.

We see the command "go to work" everywhere throughout the Bible. God says go and preach the gospel to the uttermost parts of the earth. He told Nehemiah to go and rebuild the walls, sent Jonah to go and prophesy to Nineveh, commanded Moses to go to the Promised Land, dispatched Saul to destroy the enemies of God, warned Lot to get out of Sodom, and chose Samuel to go and serve Him as prophet to the people. All of these men had one thing in common: they were to go to work in what God had called and prepared them to do.

He has prepared you as well, with talents and the opportunity to use those talents for His glory. Anybody can go and get a job, but it takes wisdom and the direction of the Lord to fulfill the work He has called you to do. Don't know what He has for you? Ask Him. Don't think you have the capability to accomplish what He tells you to do? Ask Him to help you accomplish it. Moses did. Moses complained that he wasn't eloquent in speech, so God told him to take along his brother, Aaron, who was persuasive in speech. Even the disciples did not understand the full plan for Jesus on Earth until it was accomplished, but they too were equipped and trained by God to fulfill the work He called them to do. Nowhere will you find that God spoke to one of His people and told them to just hang out, sing hymns, live off the labors of others, and wait for the eastern sky to split. He tells us to go to work and occupy until He returns. This applies not only to spiritual work and obedience but to our everyday lives as well. It is this kind of integrity and desire to know and get busy about the plans God has for you that will cause many to survive these last days.

Too many in our society today are willing to sit on their laurels while the rest of us do the work. Our children are literally being taught this in schools; hard work and merit are no longer celebrated. Instead, "community grades" or no grades at all drain away any drive our children may have for accomplishment. Let's face it—if there is nothing to accomplish, then what is the worth of doing anything? If there is no reward for the work, then why work at all? Worse yet, we have an entire generation in this nation that we have paid to literally do nothing. We pay farmers not to grow crops, we pay welfare recipients to sit and watch color TV, and we pay bureaucrats to do nothing more than make it harder for those who DO work! We often don't adequately punish those who steal from someone else's work. Work avoidance has become so inculcated in our culture that cheating has become an epidemic on the campus and in the workplace. Students and employees alike are looking for opportunities to gain without hard work.

Simply put, my friends, we have a lot to accomplish. There is a world that needs to be set right by our godly example. The good news is that we have been equipped to complete the tasks we are given. The Lord will always meet our needs, but He fully expects us to do His will—and that requires work. He will provide the necessary tools and finances, but we must be obedient and *use* the marvelous faculties He has bestowed upon us. The gray matter between our ears is there for a purpose. I note that throughout Scripture God did mighty things through people. I believe that God honors our obedience and prospers that obedience.

Let's look at a few examples. When Elisha came upon the woman and her son, who were about to eat their last meal during the drought, he instructed them to take what little they had and make them all something to eat. They took what they had set aside, and God multiplied it to them throughout the drought. They did not go hungry. Three times in the New Testament, Jesus took what someone with forethought had prepared and multiplied it many-fold to feed the masses. The boy had the forethought to bring lunch with him when others had not. When Joseph listened to the Lord, he began preparing Egypt for the famine. He went to work with other laborers to build storehouses to hold enormous harvests of grain. As a result, Joseph's work and obedience were used to save not only the Egyptians but the nation of Israel as well. These are all examples of how obedience, work, and God-given talents were used to the glory of the Lord. God blessed His servants' obedience and multiplied the work of their hands. They freely gave themselves and what they had but not with any anticipation of a return on some sort of "spiritual investment." Solomon chose wisdom over riches, and God gave him both as a result. Again, we see that all we need is supplied by the Lord, but we are not to be "spiritual welfare recipients." We are to go to work and be doers of the Word.

Let me ask those in "full-time" ministry: Are you there for a career or as a calling? Did you hear from the Lord, or are you hiding out in the "spiritual ghetto," letting someone else take care of you and your family? I realize those are pretty tough questions, but you need to be honest and ask yourself why you really are in the ministry.

Go to Work; Don't Just Get a Job

Let's look at one more aspect of work in Scripture. It says "go to work," not "get a job." I fully realize that not everyone is going to start his own business, and that it is essential for employers to have employees to make their operations work. However, I also want to be clear: we are to be all that we can be—in all that we do—for the glory of God. Colossians 3:22-24 is very clear about our responsibility to God with regard to our work and our work ethic. "Servants, obey in all things your masters according to the flesh; not with eyeservice, as menpleasers; but in singleness of heart, fearing God; and whatsoever ye do, do it heartily, as to the Lord, and not unto men; knowing that of the Lord ye shall receive the reward of the inheritance: for ye serve the Lord Christ" (KJV).

Obviously, we all have to make a living, hopefully in something we love, but the work should be to the glory of the Lord. If you work in a secular environment, be salt and light to those around you—not just in word but also in deed. Let those around you see you working to the glory of your Lord. You have work because your Lord makes sure you can provide for your family, so thank Him by giving your all to your employer. Likewise, employers need to demonstrate the power of God in their lives as a testimony to their employees. I can assure you that I am as human as anyone. I have my good and bad days in achieving these goals, but it is something we are all commanded to strive for. No ifs, ands, or buts.

Now if you are in a job that you dread to go to, or in a business that no longer interests you, then consider the words on a picture we have in our office. It is titled "Loyalty," and the words are as follows:

> If you work for or with a person, in Heaven's name speak well of them, and stand by the institution they represent.... Remember, an ounce of loyalty is worth a pound of cleverness.... If you growl, condemn and eternally find fault, why not resign your position.... But as long as you are a part of the institution, do not condemn it...if you do, the first high wind that comes along will blow you away, and probably you will never know why.
>
> —ANONYMOUS

Simply put, if you are unsatisfied in what you are doing, pray about where the Lord would lead you. Now, let me be absolutely clear: we all have days when we wonder why we are working and doing whatever it is we are doing. That is human nature. But we all need to ask if we are accomplishing what God has called and equipped us to do for His kingdom. For many, the answer will be a resounding *yes*. For some, this question will cause you to go to your knees and seek His will in your life. I am not suggesting that we all must find employment as pastors, missionaries, Christian educators, and other vocations funded and directly supported by the church. The truth is, all believers are called to be serving God in all they do, irrespective of the job description. What I am saying is that you need to look at what you are doing and ask the Lord if that is where you are to be. If not, ask for the wisdom to hear His voice and be obedient to whatever change He may bring. I truly believe that our God opens and closes doors for His purposes.

As for me, I fully expected to be a corporate or tax attorney. My reasoning was rather simple: I had never met a poor one. I realize now that was pretty selfish, but that was before the Lord showed me His way and His direction in my life. I was in New Hampshire for the presidential primary election and was standing outside a polling place when a fellow from the opposite party—probably a good ten or fifteen years older than I was at the time—came up, holding a sign representing his far Left-wing candidate. Because this was a primary, with Republican vs. Republican and Democrat vs . Democrat, this fellow and I had no argument on that day. Ultimately, however, the conversation led to his candidate, and in what seemed like a few moments, I used my powers of persuasion to demoralize this fellow with regard to his chosen candidate.

He turned and walked away like a beaten man, dragging his sign behind him. I could have relished my "victory" as a pre-law student, but surprisingly, all that came to mind was a remembrance that the tongue is like a two-edged sword and life and death come from it. Immediately, I felt a great deal of remorse for having used my wit and tongue to verbally defeat this man with whom I had no personal issue. I also began to wonder if, as an attorney, I could do such a thing daily and still live with myself. Please don't get me wrong; I have a good number of friends who are great attorneys. My dilemma was whether *my* intent in using a talent with words was for good or for evil. I had been in pre-law studies, but I returned to work and school with a decision to make. This was a moment when God got my attention through what I now know to be the voice of the Holy Spirit.

I finished college with a degree in business and ultimately an MBA, but I did not go to law school. God changed my direction—*for His glory*. Today, I get to use that wit and quick reaction daily on radio stations across the nation and around the world—hopefully, to God's glory and for His purposes as we help believers and nonbelievers alike understand the economy, politics, and current events. It is not a place where I would ever have envisioned being today, but I am grateful that God loves me enough to steer me in the right direction. He is willing to do that for all of us if we are willing to be obedient to His call.

Working for the Lord

Finally, with regard to working for the Lord, let us get past the stale terms that divide the body of Christ: *laity vs. professional*. I dare say that the apostles never considered themselves "professionals," even though they had been personally called into service by Christ Himself. Even though his call had been startling and dramatic, the apostle Paul was noted for working at a craft while ministering. His written words reveal that he did this so as not to be a burden financially on the churches in various places he traveled to as he preached the gospel. This is not to say you need to keep your pastor or church staff poor, all working a second job to make ends meet. The sad truth (especially in the Western Hemisphere) is that the church—for far too long—has left our salvation and the work of the ministry to the "professionals." We only have to take a cursory glance at the Bible to see that relatively few are called to full-time ministry, but that *all* of us are called to do the work of the ministry in some capacity. Again, remember that a believer's service at all levels of involvement should be seen as a calling, not as a "career." Again, we need to *go to work*, not *get a job*.

Scripture clearly states that those who are preachers and teachers are held to a higher standard because they are accountable to God for the flock He has entrusted to them. Let's not forget, however, that ultimately we all must stand before the Lord, who will judge our works individually in light of our obedience to what He has called us to do. Men, it is *we*—not the pastor of our church—who has responsibility for spiritual leadership of our families. Husbands and wives are entrusted with kingdom work that starts right at home.

I am challenged constantly to seek His perfect will in my life and the life of my family, and I must tell you He has never led me astray. Only my disobedience has ever led me in the wrong direction. But even in those circumstances, God is faithful to show me the way to His will for my life. My dad used to tell me growing up that our lives are often like ships on the ocean and that God is the rudder. The ship has to be in motion for the rudder to be of any use. So get off your pretty side and start doing something for the Lord. As long as you are willing to seek His face and His wisdom daily, you will go exactly where He desires you to go and work for His glory. The blessings in doing this will show themselves so strong in your life that you won't have to worry about what the government is doing about the money problem or if your family will be safe when the economy collapses. God will provide for those who fear Him and obey Him. The world will come to you looking for answers. We are His vessels on Earth no matter where we find ourselves. Once we belong to Christ, it is all about Him and not about us. At the same time, God is consistently gracious, and as we work for His glory, He abundantly, faithfully blesses us and those around us. What better endeavor could we ever find than to be in daily service to the sovereign God of all creation?

PART 2
POLITICS

CHAPTER 8

GOVERNMENT AND THE ECONOMY

What Can and Should Government Do?

By Larry Bates

I N MID-2008, I WAS OBSERVING A TELEVISION NETWORK NEWS clip showing then presidential candidate U.S. Senator John Edwards of North Carolina passionately saying, "This is President Bush's recession, and he's got to take ownership of it."

This misguided statement by a U.S. senator shows the depth of ignorance on the part of government leaders who, even if they could do something to create wealth for everyone, don't even know how our economic system works.

Richer or Poorer

Austrian economist Ludwig von Mises said, "Government cannot make man richer, but it can make him poorer." Government does not produce even one bushel of wheat or even one barrel of oil. Government can only take from those who are productive and give to the beneficiaries of the politician's choice. When government spends money for social programs, economic stimulus programs, or to fight wars, it must either tax, borrow, or print the money— there's no other way to get it. Raising taxes and expanding the size and scope of government only stymie economic growth. Tax cuts spur economic growth and even produce more tax revenue over the long haul. Borrowing by government to fund a deficit competes with the private sector for available capital. As the deficits get larger, the Federal Reserve (a private bank) will step in and monetize the debt with Federal Reserve notes, those bills in our wallet that we call money.

I have provided for you a glimpse of what British economist John Maynard Keynes, considered to be the principle architect of our current economic system, meant when he proclaimed in his book *The Economic Consequences of the Peace*, "By a continuing process of inflation, government can confiscate, secretly and unobserved, an important part of the wealth of its citizens."[1]

Keynes goes on to say, "There is no surer, no more subtle way to overturn the existing basis of society than to debauch the currency. It engages all the processes of economic law that come down on the side of destruction and does so in a manner that not one person in a million can recognize it."[2]

Immediate Problem

Economic slowdowns will reduce tax revenues to government at every level. At the federal level, it is estimated that every 1 percent increase in unemployment will add $60–80 billion to the deficit due to government spending on "entitlement" programs and loss of tax revenue resulting from the economic downturn. The president is faced with monumental political and economic challenges as the economy will face no brief dip.

America faces a dry period that could well taint the Obama administration and Democrats if President Obama does not use the power to quickly implement more tax cuts. Expect the Federal Reserve (not federal and with doubtful reserves) to continue to print more money to keep the banking system from collapsing. The Federal Deposit Insurance Corporation (FDIC) is warning of credit problems in banks due to nonperforming loans made during the recent go-go years of easy money and stock market boom and real estate debacle. There is some indication evidenced by recent bank closings that the FDIC is strictly adhering to the $250,000 insurance limit and allowing customers with amounts over the "insured limit" to take their losses—or wait for a "bank liquidation dividend."

Chickens Coming Home to Roost

The monetary excesses of the past few years are coming to light. The economy, much like an alcoholic on a binge, has been "feelin' good" over the past several years, and as in any excess or distortion of reality, there is always a "hangover" period. During this "hangover," economically called a recession, there is always some pain and a cry for more "drink" to get the new "high" going.

Historically, many representatives in Congress have become the "liquor dealers" to help their constituents out of the hangover phase. This time will be no exception as politics and political careers are at risk. Real leadership will tell the folks the truth. President Bush appeared at the outset to be doing just that—telling the truth about the true condition of the economy. Democratic leaders, meanwhile, were complaining that his telling the truth was not fair to the economy and was a ploy to pass a tax cut. Believe it, folks; this about-to-be-messy economy is real.

How Will You Be Affected?

Let's never forget that money is the key here. Government spending involves money. Tax cuts involve money. The Federal Reserve controls the money. It is money that is the wealth transfer agent in any economy around the world. Since 1971, every economic problem, crisis, or crash has been currency based. Yes, a currency crisis—and this one will be no different. It will be a currency crisis.

In 1944, the Bretton Woods Conference produced the IMF (The

International Monetary Fund), the World Bank, and an agreement that all of the currencies of the world would "float" against the U.S. dollar, and dollars were redeemable in gold at the last official price at the U.S. Treasury or Federal Reserve (a private bank). The last and present "official" price of gold is $42.22 per ounce. This is the basis the Federal Reserve (a private bank) uses to list its 262 million ounces of gold on its balance sheet ($11 billion).

History Lesson

It has been said that what we learn from history is that we don't learn from history. A bit of history will help us understand the current economic problem that is upon us and how wealth will be transferred once again.

During the late sixties and early seventies, the United States was involved in a very unpopular military action in Southeast Asia, called the Vietnam War. Whether government is financing a war or social programs, it can only get the money by (1) taxing, (2) borrowing, or (3) printing it. It was politically impossible to get a consensus to raise taxes for the war, and economically impossible to borrow the funds without collapsing the economy by soaking up all the available capital to finance the war.

The only option left was for the Federal Reserve to print the money and monetize the debt. This, of course, amounted to an increase in the number of dollars in circulation (money supply), and it diluted the value of everyone's dollar-denominated paper assets such as cash, CDs, savings, bonds, stocks, etc. This affected not only Americans but foreigners holding dollars as well. It was foreign governments and foreign central banks whose initial actions precipitated a currency crisis in 1971.

Remember the Bretton Woods Agreement, where dollars were redeemable in gold at $42.22 per ounce? When these foreign central banks and governments saw the market price of gold moving upward toward $65 per ounce, they started dumping dollars (Federal Reserve notes) for gold at the Federal Reserve at $42.22 for each ounce of gold, then selling the gold for $65 per ounce for roughly a 50 percent increase.

At this rate, the U.S. Central Bank was about to lose all of its gold. Richard Nixon was president at the time, and he had two choices: (1) Raise the official price of gold to the level of the market price of $65 per ounce, thereby officially devaluing the dollar by 50 percent, or (2) repudiate the Bretton Woods Agreement, close the gold window, and unofficially devalue the dollar.

For political reasons, Nixon chose the second option because, as Keynes put it, "There is no surer, no more subtle way to overturn the existing basis of society than to debauch the currency. It engages all the processes of economic law that come down on the side of destruction and does so in a manner that not one person in a million can recognize it."

Since 1971, the dollar and all other paper currencies have been floating against each other like boats on the ocean of the economy. All of these paper currencies are sinking; some are just sinking faster than others. This is why we saw the jump in inflation and precious metals' prices.

Looming Crisis

The day of reckoning for the U.S. dollar has simply been deferred for several years now. The dollar has been propped up artificially by an illusion of prosperity in the U.S. economy, and our "prosperity" has been financed in large part by money borrowed from foreigners.

Proof of this statement is evidenced by our massive $900 billion-plus trade deficit, and foreigners are financing this by accepting our IOUs (Federal Reserve notes) in return for their goods and services. As I recently spent a couple of weeks in Asia, it was evident that Asians are skeptical of the dollar's continued strength and are moving to sell dollars in favor of other currencies, including gold and silver.

Quite frankly, I believe that the events of 1929 and 1971 were but dress rehearsals for what is about to hit those holding dollar-denominated paper assets such as CDs, bank savings, money funds, bonds, etc. It has been a great big game of musical chairs for more than a decade now, where we have more debt than money to pay the debt (like more people than chairs). As in musical chairs, the game is over when the music stops and you haven't found your chair. The same principle exists in the economy, where those depending on the "music" to continue with business as usual are caught by surprise and unprepared when the "music" of reassuring babble stops. That reassuring babble, by the way, is the only glue holding the U.S. economy together.

This coming dollar crisis, as Keynes says, will "overturn the existing basis of society," which in plain language means that today you have money that has value and purchasing power—and tomorrow you don't.

Money is the wealth transfer agent of all times, and fiat paper money is totally dependent on confidence (con game) in the political and economic stability of the country whose currency you are holding.

Is There a Solution?

Is there a permanent, lasting solution to our chronic economic ills that come about with each business cycle? Yes. There is a direct relationship between the health and viability of an economy and the size and scope of government. We saw in the extreme case of the collapsed Soviet system where, in the waning days of the USSR, the talk among the workers was, "They pretend to pay us and we pretend to work."

In the year 2009, it was estimated that the cost to companies to comply with government regulations averaged approximately $2,500 for each worker. Part of the solution is to stop using tax policy for social engineering and "stimulus" programs where certain activities are encouraged and others are discouraged. Such actions come from the misguided view that government should manage the economy.

Such a view exists today where Wall Street is, through their army of lobbyists, attempting to get legislation that will boost the markets. Congressman Ron Paul (R-TX), a ranking member of the U.S. House Banking Committee, supported President Bush's plan to eliminate double taxation of stock dividends and said, "While tax cuts are always good for the economy, it's dangerous to promote the idea that government can create value in the financial markets. The collapse of stock prices in the last two years provides stark evidence that the Federal Reserve's monetary policy of the 1990s did not create lasting prosperity, and we should understand that tax policy is no different. Centralized planning via tax policy is every bit as harmful as centralized planning in monetary policy."[3]

As the financial markets are "sobering up," they are now demanding real value. Accountants and CEOs can lie on financial statements, but dividends don't lie. Stock prices not based on gains in productivity will fade as fast as they rose. Simply speculating that a company is worth something now or will be worth a certain amount in the future does not make it so. We must abandon the idea that the government can or should do anything to help the economy other than reducing the tax and regulatory burden.

Congressman Paul says, "Even in hindsight, many don't seem to understand the true nature of the 1990s Fed-created financial bubble. The prosperity enjoyed by so many companies and individuals was artificially caused by Fed policies that vastly inflated the money supply and made the cost of borrowing artificially low. Much of the 'money' made in the market and most of the astonishing paper increases in market capitalization were illusory. The economic problems created by this artificial bubble are real, and we cannot hope to insulate ourselves from the ongoing correction by tinkering with the tax code."[4]

So what should be the proper role of government in all of this? The only stimulus our economy needs is sensible government policies and a sound money system where economic growth with real productivity can flourish.

Congressman Paul says, "Politicians need to learn from the failed Fed policies of the 1990s, and stop trying to fool the markets and the American people by promising prosperity through government policy."[5]

We agree.

CHAPTER 9

BIG GOVERNMENT; SMALL ECONOMY

What Government Stimulus Really Provides

By Larry Bates

REAL UNEMPLOYMENT NUMBERS ARE RISING, AS NEARLY 17 percent of the population remains unemployed.[1] The government is only reporting 10 percent unemployment, as they do not count those who are "discouraged" and no longer seeking employment, nor do they factor the "underemployed."[2] The unemployment rate during the Great Depression peaked at just over 25 percent.[3] The only sector of the economy with full employment is the federal government, along with most state and local governments.

Astounding data emerged in December 2009 that showed the average pay for federal workers exceeded $70,000 per year.[4] That is $30,000 higher than the average private sector workers, who make on average just over $40,000 per year. You cannot stimulate the economy from the top down by growing the size and scope of the federal, state, and local governments with hopes that some of the money will trickle down to the average citizen and thereby stimulate the economy. Governments, by and large, when they exceed the roles of protector and builder of infrastructure become economic parasites that contribute nothing to the economy but only take from, stifle, and suck dry most economic activity.

Systemic in Nature

Our current economic and monetary systems are at the heart of our debacle. We have a debt-based economy and a debt-based monetary system. Plainly put, under this system nothing happens until money is borrowed into existence. This inflates the currency and ultimately causes price inflation. In fact, this economic game is rigged. That's right; it is rigged. How do we know? Again, let's hear from the master. In his 1920 book, *The Economic Consequences of the Peace*, U.S. economic architect John Maynard Keynes says, "By a continuing process of inflation, governments can confiscate secretly and unobserved an important part of the wealth of its citizens. There is no more sure or subtle way to overturn the existing basis of society than to debauch (destroy) the currency. It engages all the processes of economic law that come down on the side of destruction, and does it in a manner that not one person in a million can diagnose."[5]

Role of Bankers

Since the central bank (Federal Reserve) has a monopoly on the creation of money, nothing will happen to stimulate the economy until money is borrowed into existence. Most consumers are either unable or unwilling to borrow the bankers' money. Most bankers are scared to loan money for fear of future economic uncertainties. If consumers don't borrow and spend money, the economy is going nowhere and will stay suspended in stagnation. When the federal government spends and borrows the expenditure, such spending from the top down would do little if anything to help the economy. The money just doesn't trickle down enough to stimulate anything except increase the size and scope of an already giant bureaucracy. Either the Obama crowd and the Democrats in Congress are incredibly stupid and do not know what they are doing—or they know precisely what they are doing. Either way, they are destroying our country.

Where's the Money?

As we have previously pointed out, when the federal government spends money, it can get it in only three ways: tax, borrow, or print. The Obama budget is right at $4 trillion.[6] If the Feds took 100 percent of all income of those in America that make $500,000 or more, you will have raised only $1.3 trillion. This means the middle class will have to be taxed even more.

The fact is, you cannot build a European-style socialist government without European style exorbitant taxes. As in Europe, this means reduced economic activity and much higher unemployment. Deficit spending equals tax hikes and currency depreciation due to Federal Reserve printing of more money.

More Mortgage Problems—Prime Loans

In addition to the commercial real estate woes, the percentage of U.S. home owners who owe more than their house is worth will double to almost 50 percent from 26 percent reported earlier in 2009.[7] In an August 5, 2009, Reuters News Service wire report by Al Yoon states, "Home price declines will have their biggest impact on prime 'conforming' loans that meet underwriting and size guidelines of Fannie Mae and Freddie Mac, according to a report issued by Deutsche Bank."[8]

Prime conforming loans make up more than two-thirds of all mortgages and are typically regarded as less risky because of stringent underwriting requirements. The impact on the U.S. economy will be significant given that this sector of loans has the largest share of outstanding loans in the overall mortgage market. This will further fuel a vicious cycle of defaults and foreclosures as home owner equity is eliminated and the incentive to pay and stay in the home diminishes. The greater the negative equity, the more likely are defaults as chances for recovery diminish.

We Have Change, but Is There Any Hope?

To have any hope, we must change Congress and the White House. Franklin D. Roosevelt embarked upon the same plan that Obama and company are implementing, and he prolonged the Depression for ten more years. It also took twenty-five years for the stock market to just break even with precrash levels.

We interviewed Congressman Louie Gohmert (R-TX) in the first quarter of 2009, and he proposed implementing a moratorium on taxes for two to three months.

He couldn't get the proposal off the ground due to opposition from the Democratic leadership. His plan would work, and here's why. If you eliminate taxes (withholding, FICA, and Medicare) for two to three months, this would put an extra $600 to $700 in the pockets of the average worker for each month of the program. This would be the greatest stimulus you could give an economy, because it quickly gets money into people's hands. They will spend, save, or pay off debt, and the velocity (speed at which money turns over in the economy) will revive economic activity. Problems will arise for politicians when the two- to three-month moratorium on taxes ends. The masses will realize they can spend the money better and wiser than the government, and all politicians who don't agree with the masses will find themselves unemployed.

Economic and Political Risk

The greatest economic risk we face is currency depreciation due to massive printing of money to cover government spending. The greatest political risk we face is rising taxes and increased government controls over every aspect of our lives. In view of our current assessment of the ongoing economic and political crisis, we make the following recommendations:

1. Pay no attention to the advice of financial advisers who do not understand our debt-based economy and debt-based money systems. They will only understand what their bosses on Wall Street tell them. Their job is to get you into debt-based paper IOUs or some mutual fund.

2. Avoid holding bonds due to credit risk and currency depreciation. Bonds are guaranteed certificates of confiscation.

3. Do not be tempted by the pitch to get into global stocks. Remember, this economic debacle is global, and other countries (and their shares) are experiencing the same problems as in the United States. Also, avoid the pitch to get into the "green" or Copenhagen trade investments. It is a trap.

4. Avoid the pitch to invest into emerging markets. The first wave of bad news in other sectors will dry up funds for emerging markets, and you may have to wait for years to recover your investment.

5. Be more concerned with return of assets than with return on investments. Risks lurk around every corner in the investment world, and remember, "cash at the crash will be king." That's cash in CDs and money funds and cash in gold and silver coins.

CHAPTER 10

WHERE'S THE STRUGGLE?

Communism/Socialism vs. Capitalism

By Larry Bates

I N ORDER TO UNDERSTAND BASIC ECONOMICS, WE MUST FIRST put away some serious misconceptions that have been perpetuated, mainly out of ignorance, but in some cases by deliberate disinformation.

One of the serious misconceptions is that we are in a struggle between communism and capitalism. There is, in fact, only one economic system in a modern world, and that happens to be capitalism. To understand this truth, we must distinguish between capital goods and consumer goods. Consumer goods are the clothes we wear, the food we eat, the roof over our heads, and anything else that satisfies a human desire or need. Capital goods, on the other hand, are the means of production. In other words, capital is the manufacturing plants and equipment, tractors in the field, trains, plans, trucks, computers, etc. I am sure we all agree that all of the above capital goods are present in communist China and even Cuba. Therefore, these countries with a communist government are, in reality, capitalist countries. So where is the struggle?

The struggle is between monopolistic capitalism, which we see in communist or other totalitarian countries, and competitive capitalism, which we have previously known in the United States.

Unfortunately, we do not get to vote directly on this issue of choosing competitive capitalism or monopolistic capitalism. If we did, I believe there would be no contest, as most people would embrace competitive capitalism.

So what determines whether we have competitive capitalism or monopolistic capitalism? It is determined by our political system. We vote indirectly for the type of economic system we get by whom we elect to public office and by what their political views are. Originally, our U.S. Constitution and Bill of Rights insured a permanent system of competitive capitalism. However, legislation and judicial activism have ignored the tenets of the Constitution and have moved us toward a somewhat monopolistic system of capitalism.

CHART A: ECONOMIC SYSTEMS			
CAPITAL = MEANS OF PRODUCTION			
Monopolistic Capitalism vs. Competitive Capitalism			
Monopolistic Capitalism		Competitive Capitalism	
Capital held privately or by State and controlled by a few or by the State. High prices; poor quality		Capital held and controlled privately. Low prices; high quality	
Forms of Monopolistic Capitalism			
Communism	Socialism	Nazism	Fascism
ALL capital owned by the State	MAJOR capital owned by the State	SOME capital owned by the state	NO capital owned by the State
ALL controlled	ALL controlled	ALL controlled	ALL controlled

You can see in Chart A the characteristics of both competitive capitalism and monopolistic capitalism. In the same chart you will see the forms of monopolistic capitalism.

As I previously mentioned, the political system determines which economic system you have—monopolistic capitalism or competitive capitalism. Communism, therefore, is just one form of monopolistic capitalism, as is socialism, Nazism, and fascism. All of these are allowed by some form of totalitarian type of government, or by a movement toward more government dependency and control.

CHART B: POLITICAL SPECTRUM				
Monarchy	Oligarchy	Democracy	Republic	Anarchy
Rule by ONE	Rule by ELITE	Rule by MAJORITY	Rule by LAW	Rule by NONE

In Chart B you will observe a true political spectrum. On the left you have totalitarian government. On the far right you have anarchy, or no government, and in the center you have limited government. For all practical purposes, a monarchy, or dictatorship, does not exist in the world today. Modern-day totalitarian governments are oligarchies, or rule by the economic and political elite. A totalitarian system of government has generally been perpetuated by a ruling class handing down rule to chosen successors, or by democrats promoting democracy and getting the permission to rule by promising their "subjects" all types of goodies and gifts from the public treasury.

Democracy Will Self-Destruct

Over two hundred years ago, a British professor by the name of Alexander Fraser Tyler observed that "a democracy is a temporary and transitional government on the way to totalitarian government." Tyler said, "A democracy can only last as long as, and until, a majority of the people discover they can vote themselves largesse (large gifts) out of the public treasury; and then they will continue to elect the politicians promising the most. The end result is always a fall of the democracy due to economic ruin and chaos."[1]

In America, the Democratic Party is moving us toward socialism at about one hundred fifty miles per hour, and the Republicans are going only fifty to sixty miles per hour, trying to keep from looking like ogres or "uncaring" politicians.

If I hold a gun to your head and demand you empty your wallet for me, I can go to jail under the laws of any state or province in the world. However, send me to Congress, and if I pass a bill that empties your wallet, I'll probably get reelected by the people to whom I gave your money! Stealing is stealing, regardless of the name you give it.

Age of the Lie

On several occasions, I have been both amused and dismayed by comments of religious leaders in the United States embracing socialist governmental policies. On one occasion, I observed a wire service story where the head of one of the largest Christian TV networks said that "Jesus was a communist" and that the early church was "a model of communism." I thought this surely was an off-the-cuff remark made while pandering to the communist Chinese leaders while in Beijing. But later, I saw other instances where that individual was professing the same thought in writing.

We know that Jesus was not a communist when we read the account of the young man coming to Jesus, saying, "Master, speak to my brother, that he divide the inheritance with me. And he said unto him, Man, who made me a judge or a divider over you?" (Luke 12:13–14, KJV).

Jesus was not offering a grand welfare scheme to get people out of the slums and ghettos. Rather, He spent His ministry walking those squalid streets and paths from one end to the other to get the slums out of the people! He was not a communist. We also know the early church was not a model of communism, as some religious leaders have stated, because communism is *forced* community—whereas the early church was *voluntary* community. Also, God was on the throne in the early church, and under communism, government is king.

Yes, there is a difference. This lie is perhaps being perpetuated in seminaries and ecumenical circles where they are teaching "liberation theology"—where they use Christian symbols of theology but promote a Marxist view of history.

Origin of Our Current Problems

All of the economic and political debate centers around money and power, and we can trace this debacle all the way back to the Garden of Eden. When we got booted from paradise because of sin, the "free lunch" ended and we had to go to work. Labor in itself is pain, and it is natural that we want to avoid pain. Man, over the centuries, has devised schemes to live and consume off the labors of other people. That is the origin of plunder. Currently, we have become more sophisticated in our plunder, and we even now plunder under the cover of law to legitimize it. An uninformed media then glorifies it, and an apostate church blesses it.

Think about it—every war in history, every border dispute, every dissension has been over money and power. This brings real meaning to the words of God through the prophet Hosea: "My people are destroyed for lack of knowledge" (Hos. 4:6, KJV).

There is one inescapable fact: The government that can give you everything you desire must take everything you have to pay for it—including your freedom. When government spends money on a program, regardless of how "just" or "helpful" the program is, it has only three ways to get the money: (1) tax it; (2) borrow it; or (3) print it.

When the government raises money through taxes, you have less to spend as you desire. Instead, you must yield to the "wisdom" of the politicians who will spend it on the beneficiaries of their choice.

When the government borrows the money, they amass debt (i.e., national debt) and compete with businesses for available capital. Overall borrowing is limited to what others save.

When the government prints the money, this fulfills the very definition of inflation: the value of our current paper monetary assets is diminished.

Economic Illusion

A few years ago, politicians said we are living in the strongest economy in fifty years, but I want to remind you that we were living in an illusion of prosperity that was being financed with borrowed money. This "phenomenon" caused the tax revenues to increase and the budget deficit to decrease, but our trade deficit (balance of payments) is out of control with an annual deficit of over $400 billion. This means we have imported $400 billion more in goods from foreigners than we have shipped to them, causing jobs to be exported. We have paid for these imported goods with newly created credit money (borrowed), and all is well until the foreigners determine, as they have been doing the past several months, that our dollars aren't worth as much as they used to be. This is why we saw a rise in crude oil prices and other general price increases. Yes, this is inflation that has resulted in the creation of more money and credit.

We have seen only the beginning of our economic problems. Expect them to continue for a few years.

When the U.S. dollar begins to fall dramatically, the Federal Reserve will be forced to raise interest rates to keep the dollar from collapsing. The rising interest rates will affect the stock, bond, and real estate markets negatively. Unemployment will rise, prompting cries for more government programs to "ease the pain." Remember, when government spends money, they must tax, borrow, or print. The more government involvement and control, the faster we move toward a socialist type of totalitarian government.

Socialism is defined in *Webster's New World Dictionary* as "the stage of society in Marxist doctrine, coming between the capitalist stage and the communist stage, in which private ownership of the means of production and distribution has been eliminated." A communist can therefore be defined simply as "a socialist with your gun"! This is why we see a major push for gun control. Tyrants cannot safely rule an armed populace.

What Shall We Do?

First of all, we must make sure that we are not dependent upon the politicians and government for our sustenance. As tougher times come to the U.S. economy, people will cry out for government-sponsored aid. They will continue to elect the politicians promising the most, with the result that the nation will fall due to economic ruin and chaos.

No, we are not "doom and gloomers." We're excited about the future for those who understand the times and have taken, or will take, steps to storm-proof their assets against the coming ravages of government and economic crisis.

Move immediately to reduce your debt, sell excess real estate holdings, reduce or eliminate stock and bond market exposure, and get more liquid in money market funds and precious metals. If you haven't already done so, move immediately 30 to 35 percent of your total assets into gold and silver coins.

Get right, get real, and get ready. I have only outlined the condition of the economy and political system in natural and obvious terms. When you factor in God's impending judgment, it won't be a pretty picture. God has a real track record for tearing down idols. "It's the economy, stupid" has been the U.S. rallying cry in political circles and has become the idol of many Americans. This is why knowledgeable, God-fearing people must act immediately to avoid the greatest financial wipeout human history has ever witnessed.

CHAPTER 11

RHETORIC VS. REALITY

How the State of the Union Address
Influences the Future of Our Nation

By Chuck Bates

OST OF US ARE AWARE OF—AND TUNED IN, TO SOME
degree—to the annual speech delivered by the president
to a joint session of Congress. It's generally referred to
as the State of the Union Address. Some of us watch to dissect every
word and nuance, while others just watch because their regularly
scheduled program is being interrupted on most of their favorite
channels. Regardless of which category you fall into, it is important
to realize that traditionally this is the occasion when the president
lays out the framework of his vision for the nation—and that vision,
or plan, will certainly affect you and your family.

By way of speeches that have ranged from five minutes (George
Washington) to over two hours (Harry Truman), the nation has
been privy to the vision held by the individual who at that point
held the highest political office in the land. Some of these presidents
have spoken during a time of war, others during peace, but all share
something in common: the ostensible purpose of these addresses
was to convey to the American people what they had planned for
the future of this country. In the last one hundred years, however,
these addresses have had more to do with politics than with the
actual business of the nation. That said, it is critical that we read

between the lines to fully grasp what is being said and to understand what the president has in mind for the future of our nation—and ultimately, for our families.

Analyzing Barack Obama's State of the Union

Let's look at the most recent State of the Union Address delivered by President Barack Obama. Over the course of an hour and a half, the president made some assertions, made some promises, and laid out his agenda for the coming few years. As many have done before, he used the opportunity as a sort of bully pulpit to promulgate his vision to the masses. At the same time, his highwire act included attempts to encourage his base of support while intimidating others. It is essential to have a basic understanding of current events to even attempt to understand the speeches given by presidents. In this recent speech, Mr. Obama covered issues ranging from the economy and health care to immigration, homosexuality, and foreign affairs. Here are just a few examples of what he said, along with the myths and realities of each.

1. Placing blame

Early in the address, President Obama spent time blaming the previous administration for the woes of the nation and all of the economic troubles of the day. He noted that one in ten Americans still could not find work, emphasizing that *we all must work together for a solution.*

The myth is that all of the problems were caused by someone else and that he is the great bridge builder who can unite us all in solving the problem.

The reality is Mr. Obama was a U.S. senator prior to winning the election. He was supported by some of the most polarizing people in America, such as his radical former pastor, Jeremiah Wright, and former terrorist Bill Ayers. He was part of the government that wrote and passed bills into law that allowed—and in some cases *forced*—organizations such as Freddie Mac and Fannie Mae to adopt strange and highly imprudent business models, which created the real estate bubble and set in motion the Wall Street collapse of 2008. As a matter of fact, he was the second biggest recipient of campaign donations from these two groups.[1] Further, the president has all but ignored the demands of Americans from both sides of the aisle not to pursue parts of his agenda as they fear it will further harm the economy. *So much for working together.*

2. Bailouts

A few teleprompter paragraphs later, the president discussed his actions to bail out banks and his efforts to save the economy from what (without his efforts) would have been "certain destruction." Then, Mr. Obama took aim at those same banks, promising he would go after them with fees to "pay back the taxpayers who rescued them" and chastising the banks for giving bonuses to their employees.

The myth is that his administration bailed out the banks and that he had made the bailout transparent. Further, he attempted to make bank employee bonuses look bad and make punitive government fees look like a good thing.

The reality is that the Bush administration actually created the bailout plan Toxic Asset Relief Program (TARP) under the direction of then Treasury Secretary Henry Paulson. The programs have been anything but transparent, with the Federal Reserve fighting in court to conceal the names of banks that received TARP funds, and directly combating Congressional efforts to obtain information pertaining to TARP money recipients. He notes that the banks are now stabilized—but the fact is, banks are still going under every month due to many of the same factors that have been affecting them for over a year now. Government cannot really fix the matter; it can only prolong it.

Finally, the president took another swipe at the banks, using his accustomed class warfare tactics to attack banks for paying employee bonuses. For those who are not familiar with the practice, many top Wall Street firms pay their employees with a year-end bonus that actually comprises the bulk of their annual pay. Not two weeks later, the president reversed his comments, saying he was not against bonuses when two of the largest banks, who were TARP money recipients, awarded their CEOs $17 million and $9 million bonuses.

The fees Mr. Obama proposes to levy on banks "to pay back taxpayers" is utter nonsense. A "fee" is nothing but a "tax" spelled with an *f.* The banks are businesses like any others, and they will have to pass on to the consumer that new cost of doing business. So a fee on banks is really a tax on all Americans who use banks.

3. Tax cuts?

This next one really takes the cake. The president said, "Let me repeat: We cut taxes for 95 percent of working families. We cut taxes for small business.... And we haven't raised income taxes by a single dime on a single person. Not a single dime."

The myth is that this president cut taxes for all of these folks and in all of these areas and that taxes have not been raised.

The reality is that while "income" taxes have not been raised yet, the fees mentioned previously, along with Obama's proposed spending and costly added programs, will—without a doubt—necessitate higher rates. Further, the penalties coming after 2011 in the form of higher taxes on everyone will adversely affect most small businesses. Because many of them are family run, the income of the business is translated onto the owners' individual tax filings. Obama's "prosperity penalty" will thus penalize them as though they had "made a mint," when in reality most of the funds went to the operation of the business.

Additional regulation also increases the cost of government. Case in point: the president sent a proposed budget that included a placeholder for monies that *might* come in if Congress passes his cap-and-trade legislation. Most call it the "cap-and-tax" bill, as it has little to do with protecting the environment and everything to do with new taxes. The president and his advisers suggested the federal government would raise $646 billion from the program. Again this would be nearly two-thirds of a TRILLION dollars in new taxes on energy such as oil, fuel, natural gas, and electricity that would ultimately come out of your pocket and mine. That is an indirect tax hike—*and not just on the rich*, I might add.

4. Government creating more jobs

President Obama discussed the two million jobs that his administration and the Democratic Party had "saved" and "created" through their actions. He called for a new "jobs" bill.

The myth is that government can save or create any jobs (with the exception of government jobs, which are increasing in number), let alone figure out just how many were impacted by their programs.

The reality is, the administration is in total confusion on this topic. Just two days prior to the SOTU address, three different members of his administration spoke on three different Sunday talk shows and gave three different answers as to how many jobs the actions of the administration had saved. We do know that new *government* workers were hired, but as an economist, I can tell you that is a double negative to the economy. First, it takes productive people out of the available workforce and moves them into government service. Second, as the government sector balloons, the private sector will have to pay more in taxes to pay the salaries of these new government workers. Remember: the government does not produce one barrel of oil or one bushel of wheat. It can only take from those who are productive in order to pay the bureaucrats who are literally living off the rest of us.

5. Global warming

Obama again pushed for environmental legislation known as cap and trade. He applauded the House for passing its version and expressed his hope the Senate would take up the cause this year. He used the power of the bully pulpit to promote the now-discredited idea of man-made global warming by noting, "I know there are those who disagree with the overwhelming scientific evidence on climate change. Now, even if you doubt the evidence, providing incentives for energy efficiency and clean energy are the right thing to do for our future—because the nation that leads the clean energy economy will be the nation that leads the global economy."

The myth is really twofold: (1) Man-made global warming is settled scientific fact, and (2) government incentive is necessary for energy efficiency.

The reality is that there is absolutely no settled science on man-made global warming. When Larry asked Dr. William Gray (professor emeritus of Colorado State University) about global warming, Dr. Gray, one of the foremost hurricane forecasters and weather scientists in the nation, simply responded, "You will have to ask a political scientist because it really has nothing to do with real science."

Mr. Obama is so certain about the reality of man-made global warming that he wants to offer incentives to (i.e., *force*) American families and businesses to run their homes and operations by the government's rules. If you don't, you will be run out of business or forced to make significant changes in your lifestyle. Let's face it: those of you reading this material who own businesses know how hard it is to make it in today's economy. That said, if we can save a dollar here or there and run our businesses more efficiently, we are already doing that everywhere we find an opportunity. The same is true in our households.

While the president's remarks may sound reasonable, the reality is they are far from it. Under cap and trade, the costs for all forms of energy would increase. Gasoline would rise an estimated 55 percent, electricity 58 percent, and natural gas some 40 percent.[2] Further, if the "smart grid" system is ever put in place, a government bureaucrat will decide how much energy you use in your home, and if you go over your allowance (if you are even permitted to go over it), you will have to participate in a grand scheme of carbon credits (i.e., additional taxes) to pay for having used too much energy. Forget the fact that you are already paying for the energy itself. Most estimates place the burden of this legislation on the average family somewhere between $3,100 and $4,500 per year!

Because no one wants polluted air or water, private industry has already heard from its neighbors and has done a lot to make the United States one of the cleanest nations on earth. If you compare any industrial city in the United States to any industrial city in China or India, for example, I dare say the United States looks and smells a whole lot better.

At this point, let me refer you to Mr. Obama's remarks pertaining to the coal industry, made during the campaign: "What I said is that we would put a cap-and-trade system in place that is more—that is as aggressive, if not more aggressive, than anybody else's out there. I was the first to call for 100 percent auction on the cap-and-trade system, which means that every unit of carbon or greenhouse gas emitted would be charged to the polluter. That will create a market in which whatever technologies are out there to be presented, whatever power plants that are being built, that they would have to meet the rigors of that market and the ratcheted-down caps that are placed—imposed every year. So if somebody wants to build a coal-powered plant, they can. It's just that it will bankrupt them because they're going to be charged a huge sum for all that greenhouse gas that's being emitted." Those remarks cost Obama the votes of the coal states of Kentucky and West Virginia. Also keep in mind that U.S. coal is responsible for almost half the electricity produced in this nation. To run out of business a relatively clean and certainly abundant source of energy is insanity, but the president's words speak for themselves.

6. Budget surplus

Halfway through the SOTU speech the president stated, "So let me start the discussion of government spending by setting the record straight. At the beginning of the last decade, America had a budget surplus of over $200 billion. By the time I took office, we had a one-year deficit of over $1 trillion and projected deficits of $8 trillion over the next decade. Most of this was the result of not paying for two wars, two tax cuts, and an expensive prescription drug program....That was before I walked in the door."

The myths here are several: the president claims the United States had a budget surplus under Clinton; he implies that the United States asked for a war, that tax cuts "cost" something, and that our current catastrophic deficits are not his fault.

The reality is that despite the oft-claimed mantra of budget surplus under Clinton, the United States had only one month during the ninety-six months Clinton was in office when we had a surplus. You can check it out for yourself at www.treas.gov. As for the wars we have fought in both Iraq and Afghanistan, there is this indisputable fact: we were attacked on 9/11 by terrorists from the Middle East, and we went after them to curtail their ability to ever do it again. What country ever budgets money for war? Obviously, we have a defense department, which requires a defense budget, but the additional monies necessary for prolonged military action are far greater than the regular operating budget of the Pentagon.

Mr. Obama's statement that the Bush tax cuts were not "paid for" is utter nonsense. Tax cuts stimulate the economy, which then produces an increase in revenues for the government. Tax cuts "pay for themselves," by allowing Americans to keep more money in their pockets, to spend into the economy, and to increase their savings, which can be loaned out to others for new business or expansion, thus generating more tax revenue for the government. This has been proven throughout U.S. history. President Ronald Reagan proved it in the 1980s, as did President John F. Kennedy in the 1960s, Andrew Mellon (Treasury secretary) in the 1920s, and even President James K. Polk in the late 1840s. Contrary to Mr. Obama's way of thinking, tax cuts are not a *cost* to the economy; they are a stimulant to the economy. What government really *cannot* afford is tax hikes, because they damage—even destroy—the economic engine of a nation. This too has been proven: in the 1930s under Franklin Roosevelt, during the 1970s under Jimmy Carter, and currently, under Barack Obama.

Finally, the president shrugged off the catastrophic increase in the deficit during his tenure and blamed it on George W. Bush. It is true that deficits have risen under just about every administration over the last fifty years, but the deficits spurred by the actions of Barack Obama have reached historic levels. Credible economists have stated that not even our children's children will be able to pay back this colossal amount of borrowed money.

7. Deficit of trust

Let me offer just one more blatant example of rhetoric that does not match the record. About three-fourths of the way through his speech, the president said, "We have to recognize that we face more than a deficit of dollars right now. We face a deficit of trust—deep and corrosive doubts about how Washington works that have been growing for years. To close that credibility gap, we must take action on both ends of Pennsylvania Avenue to end the outside influence of lobbyists, to do our work openly, and to give our people the government they deserve."

The myth is that the president has any intention of doing or accomplishing any of the above.

The reality: All of this sounds great, and while I would agree that lobbyists have entirely too much influence on what are supposed to be *our* representatives, the president is far from honest in his call for openness in operating government. While the president talks a good game, his actions are entirely different. During his campaign Barack Obama said he would not have his administration run by lobbyists, but here are the facts: the Service Employees International Union (SEIU) president is the most frequent visitor to the White House, lobbying on issues. They also happen to have contributed over $30 million to the president's election campaign.[3] The plain truth is, the Obama administration is full of lobbyists. In the first month of his term, there were no fewer than twelve high-level positions filled by lobbyists, including the position of deputy secretary of defense and Treasury chief of staff! There are 535 members of Congress and some 30,000+ lobbyists. Most of us live hundreds or thousands of miles from where our elected representatives work, but the lobbyists live down the street from the Capitol. Barack Obama has no intention of changing the status quo in this matter.

The president is absolutely correct on one thing, however: the people do NOT trust the government anymore, and they are beginning to wake up to the reality that not all who say they are there to help have good intentions. A sea change is coming because of rampant abuse of trust on the part of politicians.

These few examples from just one speech demonstrate how important it is to know what is going on around you so that you can separate the lies from the truth. As we say on the farm, "You have to learn how to eat the hay and spit out the sticks." I have been around politics all of my life, but let me assure you that you don't need a master's degree in political science to detect a lie when you hear it. Monitor the politicians' rhetoric to see if it matches their voting records and their actions in general, and remember the adage "If something sounds too good to be true, then it probably is."

Think about what is being proposed by politicians and government officials, and run it through these litmus tests:

1. Who is going to benefit, and how is it going to be paid for?

2. Does it unequally benefit a particular group of people or businesses?

3. Is it constitutional?

4. Is it morally right in the sight of God?

We are the owners of our freedom. But like any other rare, fragile, and valuable commodity, freedom must be preserved and protected from those who would attempt to destroy or steal it. Make sure those you send to office are looking out for the next generation—not simply trying to get through the next election or weekend, whichever comes first. A better equipped, more discerning electorate could go a long way in bringing about a good "state of the union" in the years ahead.

CHAPTER 12

MEDIA TAKEOVER

Why Discerning Today's Media Is Key to Surviving the Meltdown

By Chuck Bates

T HE INTEGRITY AND OBJECTIVITY OF AMERICAN MEDIA have steadily declined over the years. Many media and news organizations are influenced by political and social groups and in turn do not represent a fair and balanced report on the serious issues that face our country. The media is something that has a significant effect on our lives. It often affects our decision making, and it certainly can mold public opinion on important issues. Whether it is television, radio, Internet, or print, media is a powerful tool—and that power can be used for good or for evil. Like money, the various mediums of communication have no character or personality of their own, but they take on the character of the people using them.

Have you ever noticed that the first things to be taken over by a tyrant or despot attempting to overthrow a country are the newspapers and the television and radio stations? The reason is simple; the various forms of media are the most effective way to communicate messages that either support or oppose the person or entities that are attempting to control a nation and its people.

Take for instance Venezuela and its president/dictator Hugo Chavez. Chavez attempted to come to power in a coup and was eventually jailed for his activities. After his release, he got a little smarter and decided he needed to "educate" the masses on why they should elect him. He promised utopia and specifically targeted discontent among the "downtrodden masses" in the rural areas and the inner cities of Venezuela. He used the media to get out his message of "change," and the result was that he won the next election.

Unfortunately, he did not stop there; Chavez then began to bully the media in his country. Eventually, he trumped up charges against some of the television, radio, and newspaper owners, threatening some with prison and simply shutting down the operations of others. Just in the space of time I have devoted to writing this book, Chavez has closed another popular opposition television channel in Venezuela, shutting down yet another venue for anyone to disagree with his policies or to broadcast their disagreement. Chavez understands the power of the media. He has even had the audacity to use the "official" newspaper of the country (a nice way of saying "state-run propaganda rag") to tell the people that the recent electrical blackouts in the nation are for the benefit of the nation. Of course, he does not want the people to realize that it has been his ineptitude and failed socialist policies that have driven away foreign investment and the best natural talent of Venezuela. That is placing the nation on a collision course with a failing electrical grid—and how will the people of Venezuela know that if there is not a free media for them to get the information?

Throughout modern history, there are hundreds of examples of dictators doing this very thing. In Rwanda, the location of one of the most brutal and savage killing sprees in history, the Hutu-controlled government killed hundreds of thousands of Tutsi and Hutu moderates after villainizing the Tutsi tribes and stirring the Hutu supporters into a frenzy, using the media of that African nation.

Hitler was a master of manipulating the media, as were Lenin, Stalin, and, to an extent, Mao. However, these latter three simply ruled with an iron fist and killed those in the media who were in opposition. In recent years, Russian journalists have often been the target of assassination to silence political opposition or to stop them from exposing corruption. Even in the United States we have seen agents of the North Korean government assault and attempt to kill dissident Korean journalists living in the United States. All of this is due to the massive power of the media; dictators are obsessed with control, and thus they abhor opposition of any kind.

While the United States may witness fewer physical attacks against the *freedom* of speech, *content* of speech is under constant assault. A great deal of what comes out of most newspapers and television news sources in the United States is biased, and the bias falls heavily on the Left side of the political spectrum. There are many conservative publications and media sources, of course, but the "controlled" media such as CBS, NBC, MSNBC, CNN, ABC, and others have a track record of promoting left-wing/socialist ideology and politicians far more than basic constitutional ideas and politicians. When it comes to the political Right, the liberal media, more often than not, smear and attack those standing up for what is based on common sense and the God-given rights guaranteed to us under the U.S. Constitution. If you find this hard to believe, then I suspect you have not watched much television in the last twenty years—or you are very naïve and lacking in discernment.

Media Biases in American Politics

Let's take a look at how you can separate the baloney from the truth—regardless of what side of the political spectrum the talking head on TV or radio may be coming from. Take a few examples of media bias. Remember when California Congressman Gary Condit was under investigation following the disappearance of one of his aides, Chandra Levy? Most news channels covered it immediately. In fairness to the former congressman, he was not guilty of anything in regards to her disappearance, but CBS anchor Dan

Rather did not even mention the story for nearly eighty-three days after it broke.[1] Being very liberal in his political beliefs and likely a Democrat, Rather did all he could to protect Congressman Condit.

Another example is the complete pass most of the controlled media have given to moral failings of a long list of Democratic politicians, while Republican politicos caught in bad behavior make immediate headlines, with calls for their resignations. Consider the treatment of Democratic congressman Charlie Rangel, as opposed to the way Republican senator David Vitter was treated by the media. Rangel is currently chairman of the House Ways and Means Committee, likely the most powerful committee in Congress. He has been under multiple investigations over his financial dealings, and in the midst of it, he has hastily amended papers and audit materials. The media have not called for his resignation as chairman of the Ways and Means Committee; instead, they have given him considerable cover by refraining from in-depth reports on his shenanigans. Senator Vitter, on the other hand, admitted to the press that he had failed his wife by visiting a prostitute. He made this announcement openly, whereupon the Leftist media attacked him mercilessly, calling for his immediate resignation and declaring that he was finished as a politician because he had betrayed the public trust.[2] Why the stark contrast in the way the media handled these two situations? Well, the answer is plain: they were giving cover to those on their side.

Another example shows us just how crazy the media bias has become in our nation. Trent Lott, the former U.S. senator from Mississippi, was practically run from office because of the following remark at the one hundreth birthday of a fellow senator: "I want to say this about my state: When Strom Thurmond ran for president, we voted for him. We're proud of it. And if the rest of the country had followed our lead, we wouldn't have had all these problems over all these years, either."[3] Thurmond came from a different era in American politics and was active during the 1960s, when racial tensions were running extremely high in the country. Just three days later, Senator Lott issued a statement of apology for a poor choice of words and for anything that might have offended anyone. But the media didn't let it drop. They went after him tooth and nail, and as a result, he was forced to leave the leadership of the Senate.

Compare that to the media treatment of liberal Democrat Harry Reid. Reid noted in a meeting (later quoted in a book) that the race of Barack Obama—whom he described as a "light-skinned" African American "with no Negro dialect, unless he wanted to have one"— would help rather than hurt his eventual presidential bid.[4] Reid also immediately apologized for the comments, and most of the controlled media gave the story as little attention as possible. Harry Reid kept his position as the leader of the Senate.

Media Biases in Finance

Let's look at bias on matters that directly affect your wallet. I cannot count the times I have heard the major networks and newspapers declare that the economy is rosy, when such statements could not be further from the truth. Typically, this is where blatant ignorance on the part of the media is used by the current administration, the Federal Reserve, and Wall Street to promote a "point of view" that serves their purposes—distortions and biases at best, and outright falsehoods at worst. Take for instance a recent article that not only supported the liberal agenda of President Obama with regard to his meddling with the economy, but also literally declared that all is well and that the economic ship had been righted.[5] That very same day, new data indicated that nearly 500,000 more Americans had filed new unemployment claims that week! Not only that, but the foreclosure rate had accelerated that month by more than 14 percent from the same month a year before—and had risen still more from the previous month![6] How can you tell a lie from the truth if the media are lying to you or simply reading the teleprompter while totally ignorant of the subjects they are reporting?

This is where discernment and good old common sense must come to your aid. These should be the first weapons in your arsenal of cutting through the mess and getting to the truth of the news. If you look down the street and you see every other house in the neighborhood up for sale or in foreclosure, you know the economy is *not* recovering. When your neighbors and friends are losing their jobs by the droves, things have *not* gotten better yet. When the actions of the president and complicit politicians actually prolong the problem, they are not fixing anything. More often than not, they're making it worse! Unfortunately, many on the left side of the aisle—and even a few on the right—are willing to lie to the American people. The liberal media are largely complicit, hoping you won't figure it out.

There is hope, however. The tide is changing as more and more news media outlets are becoming available and accessible to just about everyone. Technology has been a pretty good friend to those of us who are fed up with the old-line media and are looking for truth. The Internet, talk radio, and the availability of relatively inexpensive platforms such as cable have introduced competition, and the old guard are feeling it financially. When it was primarily just the "big three" networks of ABC, NBC, and CBS along with public television, we had little choice and there was little debate on the issues. But today I have over one hundred channels in my home, and at least twenty of them are focused on news and talk shows. Talk radio has changed the political landscape of our nation. Once President Reagan introduced competition of thought by striking down the so-called Fairness Doctrine in 1987, the face of radio changed forever. Since then, Rush Limbaugh, Marlin Maddoux, Sean Hannity, Glenn Beck, and yes, even Larry and Chuck Bates have had a medium for reaching massive numbers of people with news they would otherwise not get from the controlled media. The availability of so much immediate information has largely put newspapers out of business. Day-old news has about as much appeal today as stale bread. Have you ever been in "Jolly Old England" and bought fish-and-chips wrapped in a newspaper? So why spend money on a "fish wrapper" when you know it's going to have a Left-leaning slant on the news? The Internet has brought us almost instantaneous access to the news around the world.

Is there bias on both sides on the radio and the Net? You bet there is—but at least you now get to see all sides, and you can use your God-given wisdom and discernment to see the truth and make your own decisions.

But wait—there's a fly in the ointment. Along with this new media and increased access to information, we see the assault on free speech rearing its ugly head again. The Left, stinging from the failure of their media organs, are waging an all-out attack against your freedom of speech and freedom to listen to and view what you want to hear and see. There are calls from the Left for a rein-statement of the so-called Fairness Doctrine, where any talk show would have to give the exact number of seconds to opposing views if the show wants to be on the air at all!

Now, on our national talk show we gladly welcome the opposition to come on the air and debate their positions with us. The problem is, they know that much of what they are pushing is indefensible, so they rarely want to come on the air. Let me give you an example.

A few years ago I invited Ms. Johnnie Turner, then director of the Memphis branch of the NAACP, onto the show to discuss issues affecting the black community. She was fine for the first ten to fifteen minutes, but then I started asking the harder questions, and she got rather uncomfortable. The straw that broke the camel's back was when I asked why the NAACP and other organizations no longer were promoting real black American heroes such as George Washington Carver and Booker T. Washington, but were focusing instead on rap artists and promoting disgraced sports figures to black youth. Well, the conversation at that point was over, and Ms.

Turner's parting shot just before she hung up the phone was, "You don't tell us who our icons are!"

I was simply asking why we don't celebrate real men instead of gangsta rappers. Black kids deserve to know that, although George Washington Carver's parents were slaves and he had little education early in life, he eventually became a professor who found over three hundred uses for the peanut—a marvelous contribution to business and industry in America! And he took his scientific and agricultural expertise back to the poor black farmers in the South to help them become productive with their land and financially successful for the benefit of their families. Why would any black American hang up on me for pointing out that there are real black Americans heroes?

To be fair, I need to state that this kind of willful blindness is not reserved solely for those on the Left side of the aisle. In 2009 Larry and I interviewed a "conservative" columnist from the *Washington Times* (a fairly conservative newspaper) who also hung up during an interview on the air. Our guest was Amanda Carpenter, a young columnist and commentator. We asked her about some of President Obama's positions, and ultimately, Larry asked her a question that we had been getting from a lot of callers: "Is the president really a U.S. citizen? And if so, why is he refusing to produce his birth certificate to silence his critics?"

Well, Ms. Carpenter became agitated at the question, and when Larry pressed for an answer on the matter, we heard a click and silence on the other end of the line. We assumed she had a bad cell connection or some other technical problem, so our engineer tried several times to reestablish the connection. One of our producers attempted to contact her by phone and e-mail for two days after the interview but received no response from the guest. Perhaps we will never know what sent her running from the interview, but tough questions should be the norm for journalists and talk show hosts. Whatever happened to asking the "who, what, where, when, and why" questions?

Back to the Fairness Doctrine. The Leftists in America are

stinging from the failure of *Air America*, their attempt at talk radio. Liberals are distraught over it, and when not blaming one another for its failure, they are blaming the marketplace. "It's not fair!" "There is too much conservative radio!" "Big corporations are keeping liberal talk off the air!"

Liberal radio, just like liberal television news and newspapers, is failing because their political ideas stink! We also DO NOT need another Fairness Doctrine or other government intervention to "level the playing field." That would be an outright assault on the First Amendment right to freedom of speech and the press. As a matter of fact, National Public Radio (NPR) has far more outlets for their Left-leaning "news" programs than Rush Limbaugh does, but the free market of ideas demonstrates that people gravitate to what they like and agree with. Obviously, *Air America* isn't what the public wanted. Isn't that what it should boil down to? In my local area, the demographics are overwhelmingly black American. Consequently, there are more radio stations that broadcast rap music, black gospel, and R & B than there are stations that broadcast, for example, country/bluegrass. This is fine with me; it represents what the local market demands.

Look at it this way: If you live in an area that gets lots of snow, you are more likely to buy a four-wheel-drive vehicle. So, the local auto dealers will make sure to stock what you need and want. The same is true when it comes to consumers and news/talk radio, television, and newspapers. Government does not need to intervene unless it is trying to control the free flow of information. Sadly, this is exactly what is taking place in our nation today. It underscores the importance for all of us to practice serious discernment as to where we choose to get our information. There are crackpots on both sides of the political spectrum, but ultimately, what we should be seeking is the unvarnished truth.

It is important to educate yourself on the media and understand the assaults being made on your liberties. With regard to the attack on media freedom, let me suggest you get a copy of Dr. Kenneth Hill's book *Assault on Liberty: Rebirth of the Fairness Doctrine*. It will give you an important—and interesting—look into the history of censorship of the truth in this country. In the years following World War II, radio broadcasters who provided air time to preachers of the gospel were driven from the public forum by the federal government. The origins of the Fairness Doctrine were actually aimed at ministers, as some politicians were afraid of the influence of preachers of the gospel. It was never actually a law; it was unconstitutional, overreaching regulation by the FCC. It was implemented in 1949, and it remained in effect until it was abolished during the presidency of Ronald Reagan in 1987.

Inform yourself and others about this vitally important subject. Many on the Left believe the federal government has a right to censor media that print or air political positions that are not in sync with the political party in power. The issue has been a priority on the far-Left agenda for some time, and in light of the current free flow of information (which does not sit well with the Left), we are likely to see it surface again with renewed fury.

Debate is a healthy thing. Competition of ideas is also a very healthy exercise. When a business, church, or family is making big decisions they need to weigh all of the options. How much more important is debate when it comes to political and economic actions that affect us all? In the days ahead, nothing will be more important than the source and quality of information that you receive. Discernment is absolutely necessary. Even networks such as FOX News, typically considered somewhat conservative, get it wrong a lot of the time. Further, there are topics they simply will not give much attention to because the network's ownership has a stake in one area or another. The same is true for what we read.

I remember a number of years ago a front cover article in the money section of the *USA Today* newspaper interviewing a major mutual fund manager who declared to the paper that tech stocks were the place to invest. Six months later, this same mutual fund manager had almost completely liquidated all tech stocks from his fund. What he did, essentially, was use the article to get people to run to tech stocks, which allowed him to unload his portfolio on the unsuspecting masses who had created a market for him that he otherwise would not have had. Don't be fooled by trends or herd mentality when it comes to the media. Ask God for wisdom in all matters, and He will give it to you.

Controlled Access

One final point on the importance of the media: it is a powerful medium; therefore, don't be surprised by increasing attempts to control your access to information—especially truth and quality information. Support the advertisers and sponsors of alternative media, and vote with your feet. Walk away from those networks that lie to you day after day. I never cease to be amazed at the number of self-proclaimed Christians and conservatives who get pulled in by the lies of the media. I am really appalled by the timidity we sometimes see in conservative—and specifically ministry-oriented— media when it comes to taking a stand on what is right. If you run or work for a media ministry or own, manage, or work for a Christian television or radio station, don't live in fear. We don't serve a God of fear. Get on the offensive; after all, we have the truth of God on our side. When you play offense, you decide what the battlefield will be, how much you are going to expend on it, and when you are going to leave it. You put the enemy into confusion, cleaning up the aftermath and regrouping while you have gone on to the next battle.

For too long, righteous people have been cowed by the media and the culture. Now is the time to stand. We can't continue to live oblivious to the things that are sneaking in and threatening our ability to make sound choices about our future. National crisis is at our door, and the last thing we need is biased and controlled access to information as we navigate through these hard times. Ephesians 6 commands us to take a stand. Take the enemy on. The truth can destroy a mountain of lies.

Obviously, some will not want to hear the truth, but the majority, I believe, are inclined to agree with Patrick Henry: "For my part, whatever anguish of spirit it may cost, I am willing to know the whole truth; to know the worst, and to provide for it."[7]

CHAPTER 13

COMMIT AND OCCUPY

Debunking the Misconceptions of a Christian's Place in the World

By Chuck Bates

SOMETHING WE HEAR ALMOST WEEKLY, EITHER ON THE AIR OR in a letter or e-mail from a listener, is the misconception of a believer's place in the world—specifically, in politics and culture. It is our hope to correct these misconceptions in order to empower the followers of Christ to become active in all areas of their community and enable them to be salt and light to all those with whom they come in contact. We want to fortify Christians for action because Christ told us to "occupy" until He returns (Luke 19:13, KJV). The basic meaning of *occupy* is to do just that: dwell, take over, take possession. Unfortunately, some common misinterpretations of Scripture, reinforced by flaky teaching, have neutralized a great portion of the church to the point that they have little to no effect on the culture. And this is something we cannot afford. Our nation is in crisis, and in order for Christians to stay ahead of the curve, we must clear up these misinterpretations of Scripture and begin to live it the right way.

Obey God Over Government

One primary misconception we run into concerns the passages in Romans 13 that pertain to submitting to governing authorities. Some take this passage to the extreme and suggest that we should never so much as question government authority. Some interpret it to mean that God would be angry with us for disobeying the rulers of our day. Both of these interpretations are completely in error. Indeed, God allows things to happen and nothing catches Him by surprise, but while government, at least righteous government, is to be respected, it should not be without accountability. This misinterpretation has actually allowed some of the greatest atrocities in history to take place. Because good men idly sat by and used this passage as a reason not to get involved in the affairs of the community or the nation, genocides and the trampling of God-given rights have occurred around the globe. Note that verse 3 indicates that the government in question is of generally good repute.

What happens, though, when the evildoers are the government? What is a Christian to do when the government creates ungodly laws that run contrary to God's commands? Are we to sit by and watch it happen—or do we fulfill our marching orders to occupy the land? I think the answer is obvious: we obey God. God is not schizophrenic or double-minded. The passage indicates that a person doing good should have nothing to fear from the government, but we also know that God would have us obey His commands, regardless of what man-made government might demand. Look at the military as an example. Let's say a private in the army is given an order by a general and he comes across a colonel or captain who gives him a conflicting order. Which one does he obey? The hierarchy would demand that he obey the original order from the general, as he is ultimately the one in charge. The same is true for Christians. If government is countervailing God's commands, then the Christian has a responsibility to obey God over government.

One need only look at World War II Germany. We all are aware of the horrific genocide against the Jews of Europe carried out by Hitler and his minions. Many still wonder why the church in Germany did not stand up for what was right. The truth is that, while some did, they were silenced. Unfortunately the majority simply obeyed the government of Hitler, and in some cases they even supported his actions! That's right. I have a picture of evangelical Protestant pastors in Germany at that time literally blessing the Nazi flag! There were even churches that changed the order of service so they were singing and playing music during the times the Jewish families were being herded toward camps or trains— the music and singing tended to drown out the screaming. That is indeed a sad commentary. But is that any different from churches in the United States that fail to even protest the ungodly actions of our own government? There are large numbers of Christians who actually frown on the actions of other Christians who protest the slaughter by abortion of millions of the unborn. Still others fear being labeled "homophobic" if they challenge the homosexual movement in the country. These are the same "Christians" who will likely obey the hate crimes law that prohibits the preaching of Romans 1 but will use Romans 13 as a convenient excuse not to make a peep.

Friends, if a police officer ordered you to randomly shoot a person in a crowd, you wouldn't do it because you know it is both wrong and illegal. So why would you obey a law that is contrary to what is moral and is blatantly contrary to God's law?

Most folks who bring up the Romans 13 passage are looking for a way to get out of their responsibility to think and act. They have not come under conviction, and therefore they don't feel an obligation to affect the culture as "salt and light." There is a strong admonishment in Matthew 5:13: "You are the salt of the earth; but if the salt loses its flavor, how shall it be seasoned? It is then good for nothing but to be thrown out and trampled underfoot by men." Those strong words are from Jesus Himself.

Think about this for a moment. If we are commanded to spread the gospel to the whole world, then we have to take action to accomplish this mission. If people do not *hear* the truth, how will they *know* the truth? Consider the prophets throughout the Bible. Many times they had a word from the Lord for the king or ruler of a land. Often it was something the king did not want to hear, but the faithful prophets delivered the message and risked the wrath of the earthly leader. Consider how Moses confronted the pharaoh, choosing to obey God rather than man—even the supremely powerful man who was the pharaoh and who was thought to be a god who ruled by divine authority. (Some might say that a few U.S. presidents have had such a complex!)

Then there was Daniel, thrown to the lions because he dared to defy a law put in place by deception and for the purpose of getting rid of a political and spiritual enemy. Consider Esther, who violated the law of her day by coming before the king unannounced and uninvited so she could plead for the king to save her people from destruction. Hers was a "crime" punishable by death in that culture. Nevertheless, she obeyed the calling God had for her life, despite the potential consequences.

When man's laws conflict with the laws of God, then the Christian has only one real choice: obey God. This does not excuse the actions of someone who breaks God's law in the process of "upholding" God's law, because we know that God does not contradict Himself. Individuals who have blown up abortion clinics or killed abortion doctors are guilty of murder. But those who just sit in their pews and never take action when the laws of God are routinely violated in their society by man-made laws are guilty of disobedience to God because they are not occupying. We will talk more about this in chapter 14, "Give Me Liberty."

We have a responsibility to be involved. We are to be proactive in all areas of our society as the "salt and light" that Jesus commanded us to be.

Defending What's Yours

Another major misconception among Christians is the issue of self-defense. This misconception is often tied to the one previously discussed. The misinterpretation is that you are supposed to sit like a potted plant and die instead of defending yourself against someone attempting to kill you or do you serious bodily harm and injury. Friends, it is hard for me to believe we need to address a subject that seems to be nothing more or less than plain old common sense. However, we have had callers on our national radio program who contend that it would be better to die than to take someone else's life in self-defense. I remember one caller who equated such "self-sacrifice"—that is, allowing his life to be taken—with "witnessing" to the murderer! Even a Christian police officer from a major metropolitan area called in, confused about the same issue. I asked him if he would shoot someone in the line of duty who was endangering someone else. He responded that he would. However, the church he was attending had him so confused on the matter that when I asked if he would defend himself or his family if an armed robber invaded his home, he said he wasn't sure.

Confusion has no place in the church. God is clear that a man who does not take care of his family is worse than a heathen and has denied the faith. If God has given us life and the defense of it as a right, then by all means we had better defend it. Even Jesus told His disciples to get a sword. Now, for those who want to argue that Jesus was commanding His disciples to procure a copy of the Bible, let me set you straight. There were no Lifeway Christian bookstores, Lemstone's, or even a Scrolls "R" Us at the time. The word *sword* used in this passage specifically means just that—a sword—a metal tool used for self-defense. Throughout the Bible,

God's people carried weaponry for one reason or another. Even the Book of Exodus prescribes the "dispatching" of thieves who come in the night, as opposed to presenting them the opportunity for restitution if the thief was caught in the light of day. In other words, the home owner had the right to kill the thief who came in the cover of night.

We have a responsibility to protect our families. At this point in the argument there is usually one in the crowd who will say something like, "So you're going to kill somebody just for 'stuff' or 'physical things'?" Well, Scripture is clear on the matter, but no—I'm not going to kill someone for "things." In the real world today, however, it is rarely a simple matter of giving the thug or punk your car or wallet. All too often, a robbery victim may be the target of a gang initiation murder, or a woman may be the target of a rape. I fully expect that a true Christian is going to defend himself and his family. As to the argument that "it's just stuff"— what if your wallet contains the proceeds from your recently cashed paycheck and you are dependent on that to feed your family for that week. Is it just "stuff" then?

A couple of years ago on a beautiful May afternoon, my wife, our infant daughter, and I were traveling home from a visit with family across town. I noticed that we were being followed by a car that changed lanes every time I changed lanes. As we approached our home, I saw that the car continued to follow us. At that point I informed my wife that we had a problem. To make a long story short, it was an attempted carjacking. I say "attempted" because the bad guy discovered I was not an easy victim. I was prepared and armed with a handgun. After changing direction and getting my wife and daughter out of immediate harm's way, I had a confrontation with the would-be carjacker, who came to the sudden realization that it was time to change careers or at least find easier prey. It was no laughing matter. The point is that I was prepared, trained, and willing to defend my family. The thug was convinced of that as well. He got to live another day, and so did my family. The police never caught him, as he fled the scene, but I hope his near-death experience convinced him he should find honest work. I did become a statistic, however. That day I joined the ranks of those who defend themselves with a firearm without having to fire a shot. Dr. John Lott estimates in his studies of crime and self-defense that in the United States alone, law-abiding, gun-carrying citizens stop 2.3 million crimes per year without firing a shot.[1]

Now, some believers would take me to task for my actions, while others would applaud my actions. Bottom line: I have a responsibility to protect what God has placed in my care and stewardship. A car, money, or "stuff" can be replaced fairly easily, but my wife, my daughter, or a brother cannot. Life is a gift from God, and God gave us the right to defend it. Christians need to understand that we don't serve a baby Jesus, drooling in a manger—instead, we serve a warrior Shepherd who is coming back in a much different form and manner than He came originally.

Life is not a game, and there is no restart button in life-and-death situations. Ask Charl van Wyk what he thinks on the matter. Charl is a missionary from South Africa, who, as a result of a terrorist attack on his church, is now the author of a book called *Shooting Back*.[2] At the time of the attack, Charl was armed with a small revolver. Despite the terrorists being armed with machine guns and grenades, Charl's actions thwarted the attackers and sent them fleeing—simply because they met resistance in a Christian church. Sadly, eleven members of the church died, and fifty-eight were wounded. But because one man stood against the attack, hundreds more were saved. Furthermore, the terrorists abandoned their plans to blow up the church, as they were now fleeing for *their* lives. Evil comes in many forms, and the Christian must be prepared and willing to confront it spiritually or physically. Pacifism is not an option or an excuse.

Money Is Not Evil

One other misconception among many in the church is that money is somehow inherently evil. Often you will hear the Scripture misquoted, "Money is the root of all evil." The complete verse from 1 Timothy 6:10 reads, "The love of money is a root of all kinds of evil, for which some have strayed from the faith in their greediness, and pierced themselves through with many sorrows." Note that it is the *love* of money that is *a* root of all kinds of evil.

King Solomon wrote in Ecclesiastes 10:19, "Money answereth all things" (KJV). You see, money is inanimate. It has no nature or character of its own but takes on the character of the one using it. Money is a weapon that can be used for good or for evil. Let's face it: you can't build a church without money anymore than you can build a gambling casino without money. Money is simply another tool that we must use as good stewards. Money is one of the topics most often mentioned in Scripture, and it's something we all have to use daily; yet, it is one of the topics least understood, either out of ignorance or out of fear that money in itself is an evil thing. In other chapters of this book, as well as in Larry's book *The New Economic Disorder*, we have attempted to help believers and nonbelievers alike understand what money is, what money is not, and how to best protect it and use it for God's purposes.

Judge Not?

Finally, a big misconception among Christians is the whole concept of judging one another. I realize the topic may seem confusing, particularly in light of this seeker-friendly, politically correct world of modern theology, but let's not park our brains at the door on this one. It is true that in Matthew 7, as well as a few other passages, we are commanded not to judge one another as though we are constantly bickering over the basic things of the Scripture. However as noted by Charles Ryrie in his commentary on the matter, this

135

does not mean we may not *judge righteously* in an effort to help a brother or sister in Christ by confronting them about sin. Ryrie notes, "This does not mean that one is never, in any sense or to any extent, to judge another, for verse 5 indicates that when one's own life is pure, he should 'cast the speck out' of the brother's eye. It does mean that a follower of Christ is not to be censorious (meaning, 'harshly critical')."[3]

We also read in 1 Corinthians 2:15, "But he who is spiritual judges all things, yet he himself is rightly judged by no one." Dr. Ryrie again notes in his commentary, "The mature Christian who is led and taught by the Spirit judges all things, i.e. he can scrutinize, sift, and thereby understand all things, but unbelievers and even carnally minded Christians cannot judge (understand) him."[4]

Throughout the New Testament in particular, we see how the church is to handle the unbeliever as well as discipline a brother or sister who has departed from the faith and is going down a road of sin. That is not judging; it is simply calling it like it is. If someone in the church is departing the faith or faltering in their walk, we are not judging; instead, we are actually showing love by confronting them, helping them back on the narrow path, rebuking and correcting them if they are unrepentant. We even go so far as to disassociate them if they turn their hearts against the truth of God's Word. That takes a certain amount of common sense and judgment.

Many churches have become so seeker-friendly that they do the lost sinner a great disservice by failing to confront sin. When we fail to confront sin, we actually jeopardize the rest of the church. As Scripture warns, "A little leaven leavens the whole lump" (Gal. 5:9), meaning that if you tolerate sin, it will spread quickly, affecting many others. This idea should not be foreign to any of us. Consider your children and what you allow them to watch on television. (Most of what masquerades as entertainment these days is not appropriate for adults to view, much less our children.) We rightly judge that certain things can have a destructive effect on our children. So why do we tolerate blatant sin? Usually it boils down to a greater fear of man than a fear of a righteous God. When we look at entire "Christian" denominations that have accepted and embraced abhorrent lifestyles such as homosexuality, it is easy to see the truth of the "lump of leaven" analogy.

It is not judgment to call sin a sin. I remember a pastor friend once noted that many Christians have become worldly to the point where "they are so broad-minded they are flat headed" and "so open-minded their brains have fallen out." Common sense goes a long way when it comes to putting your Christianity in practice.

Misconceptions can cause a lot of mischief and confusion in any setting. Ultimately, the result is a neutralizing or paralyzing effect, which, if allowed to continue, can damage that organization beyond repair. Our nation's government and economic systems may be collapsing all around us, but the church need not be confused. We have the answers on all things, and all we have to do is study the Word of God and seek His guidance. It is like having an open-book test, with the teacher willing to show you the chapter and verse. We need only avail ourselves of His gracious offer.

CHAPTER 14

GIVE ME LIBERTY

Exercising Your Right and Power to Act

By Chuck Bates

I N THE UNITED STATES, WE LIVE IN A CONSTITUTIONAL republic, not "the world's greatest democracy," as is so often stated in the classroom and on the nightly news. A pure democracy is really majority rule, whereas a republic is rule by law. In a democratic-style meeting, the majority decides to do to the minority whatever they wish. In a republic, all are protected by the law. Of course, laws can be changed by the majority, but it is through a constitutional process that protects the individual's liberty. This is why it is imperative that the individual be involved in the political process. Being involved on an individual level is necessary for the maintenance of a free society and to protect individual interests and liberties. Far too many Americans, particularly those in the church, have eschewed this basic right and responsibility. They look at politics as dirty and something to be avoided. Some are just too lazy to get involved, or they claim they haven't the time. I submit that if the body needs water and food for survival, you make time for that. Why is it any different when it comes to feeding and watering your freedom and liberty?

It is true that politics can be a mean business, but that shouldn't surprise any of us. Anytime someone attempts to legislate something that takes a basic freedom from someone else, there is going to be a fight—as well there should be. When we abdicate our personal responsibility to stand up for our rights—particularly those given to us by God and not by man—we are being disobedient to God Himself. The founders of the United States were led by God in drafting both the Declaration of Independence and the Constitution. One common thread throughout these documents is that we are endowed with natural rights from our Creator. The founders called them "unalienable" rights.

Let's look at that word for just a moment. Literally, *unalienable* means "not to be separated, given away or taken away; incapable of being repudiated or transferred to another." Simply put, these are an individual's natural rights, given to us by God, and NO man can take them away. Life, for instance, is given by God, and man is responsible to defend it.

The same is true with liberty: it is the right and power to act, believe, or express oneself in a manner of one's own choosing. God in His divine wisdom gave us life as well as a free will to make our own determinations. We choose whether to serve Him or reject Him, and that choice has eternal ramifications. Throughout life, we make decisions of our own free will in the liberty given to us. Now, of course, some make poor decisions, such as committing a crime against another's unalienable rights; that is where the law comes into play. For a free people, the law is to "remain in the corner" while we practice responsible self-government and self-control. The law is to come out only when we lose sight of our responsibility to rightly govern ourselves, and we impinge on the rights of another. Because we have not exercised that responsibility in the public square, others have taken our place. Sadly, there are a great many people you wouldn't trust to watch *your dog* who are making decisions that affect *you and your family.*

The Lord has given Larry and me great opportunities over the years to see and participate in the process of government at almost every level. We have both run for public office, and Dad was an elected legislator serving on powerful committees that affected a lot of lives in areas ranging from agriculture to banking. I have worked in campaigns; been active in local, state, and federal issues; and also worked in the White House Office of Political Affairs. All of these unique experiences have given us insight into politics and the understanding that if you are not active in shaping your own destiny politically as well as spiritually, someone else will likely do it for you. You see, there are a lot of folks involved in politics for the wrong reasons. Some are there for mere financial gain, while others are there for power over the lives of others. Still others are involved because they hate the nation of laws that we live in and seek to destroy it from the inside out.

The good news is that there are also those who are involved to preserve liberty. I remember when I first decided to run for office, and Dad asked me a question that had been asked of him by a constituent in his legislative district many years earlier: "Why are you running for office?" This was a simple yet very direct question. He followed up the question with an even more direct question: "Are you running to participate in the plunder or to stop it?" I think this is a question that should be asked of every candidate, and certainly, all candidates should ask it of themselves when it comes to political action of any sort.

When I decided to run for office, I knew my reason for running was to stop the plunder and to rein in a too-big and too-powerful government. I wanted to work to insure the chance for my children— and yours—to live in a place where they have the liberty—and the power as free citizens—to pass that liberty on to the next genera-tion. But what struck me about the question, as it did my dad when he was asked the question so many years before, was that there really are only two reasons to get involved in the political arena: to participate in the plunder—or to stop it.

I did not win my two attempts at elected office, but my efforts were instrumental in stopping the passage of a state income tax.

Additionally, my campaign eventually ran a twenty-four-year incumbent—who did not even live in his district—out of office. Thus, we cleared the way for other liberty-minded candidates to eventually take that office and others. Further, it was a great learning experience and one that I have been able to put to good use over the years. The Lord opened doors for me to get involved in educating and informing people about the assaults on their liberties. Those opportunities went far beyond what I could have accomplished in that particular legislative seat.

Unfortunately, a lot of Americans—especially Christians and pastors of churches—shy away from the political arena out of fear, laziness, or ignorance. Once, my dad was talking with a fellow about the political climate of his state, and the fellow responded he didn't get involved in politics and had little reason to start. My dad asked him if he was in business, and he said yes, to which Dad replied, "Then you have a reason to be involved in politics, because I can assure you someone is involved doing things politically in your name, and it does affect you." Suddenly, this fellow realized he had a dog in the fight.

On our national radio broadcast we have a set policy: if someone calls into the show complaining about government but doesn't vote regularly, we hang up. If an individual is not willing to be part of the solution to the political ills of the day, then he has silenced his own voice. It is a great object lesson for our listeners: When we are not doing something about the problem, then we really have no right to complain when those rights are infringed. We all silence ourselves when we fail to stand for what is right and not speak or act in the defense of the liberties given to us by God. I have often noted scripture that backs up this responsibility, but one of my favorite examples is in the last chapter of Proverbs. Most know this text for the definition and description of a godly woman, but when we read verse 23, we see something that often is overlooked: "Her husband is known in the gates, when he sitteth among the elders of the land."

This tells us at least two things: he is active in what is going on in his community, and he is known by the leaders. To be known, you have to be active in your community to some extent. You have to be salt and light to all of those around you in some capacity.

Politics in the United States has become a blood sport, and with the seemingly constant expansion of government, it has become a huge business as well. As a result, a large segment of society is going to government to make a living for themselves off the labor of others. Many think of this in terms of welfare recipients, but it extends well beyond those poor families receiving aid from the government. There are corporate welfare recipients and political entrepreneurs who skim off sums of money and extravagant benefits from the labors of taxpayers—sums that make the typical welfare case look paltry indeed. A lot of businesses have found it easier to legislate themselves a living than to compete for it in the marketplace. The result is, we get to pay for it. If you stand idly by and watch, you are essentially complicit in the theft. In a typical crime, you could be considered an accessory to the crime.

Let's look at a perfect example of this type of legislative profit making. In my home state there was a doctor who invented the child car seat. Now don't misunderstand me. My family uses a car seat for our little ones, but many of you reading this book were like me, growing up prior to the days of the car seat. We all survived long enough and healthy enough to read this paragraph. The doctor was not having the success he had anticipated from his new venture, so he set off to the state capital, seeking a legislator who would hear his case and propose a bill that would eventually mandate that all parents put their children in car safety seats. Of course, the doctor made a fortune by forcing others to buy his product. Children today are likely safer for the use of the seats, but the government mandate to buy a product is an infringement on liberty. Because citizens didn't get involved at that time, this fellow made a mint off the labor of others. If his invention had simply proven itself to the public, it would likely have generated a great many sales eventually, but that choice was never allowed for the consumer. Mandating that people buy a particular product or service is never the right thing to do. My dad would ask any lobbyist who was seeking his support for a bill if the proposed legislation in any way gave someone an unfair advantage over another. If it did, he told them he would not support it. Protecting our liberty should always be uppermost in the minds of those who are elected to represent us. This is why people in office, or at the very least people involved in politics at every level, must have discernment and godly wisdom. The wisdom of God was necessary to the creation of this nation's liberty, and it must surely be necessary for the preservation of it.

How Do We Get Involved?

Well, now that we know that we have a responsibility to get involved—and that there is no excuse to get out of that responsibility—how do we go about doing it? This part is simple, my friends: *pray*. But don't stop at prayer; ask God for wisdom and direction to lead you to the issues, campaigns, or advocacies He would have you focus on. There are too many issues for any one of us to take on all of them. As a matter of fact, this is what overwhelms so many and neutralizes them; at some point, they begin to feel powerless.

Our nation has faced big battles before. Each of us has a lot on our plate, but none of us are experts on every issue or capable of handling everything that comes our way. Think with me. I am an economist by training and experience. While I do have some mechanical ability, I would not call myself a mechanic by any means! When my truck has an issue, I take it to someone who knows how to fix it. The same is true with the plumbing in my house or the roof on my office. Now, if the mechanic, the plumber, or the roofer needs a business model or economic advice, I am the guy for them to call.

You see where we are going with this? We all have talents and interests in various areas. Some people need to be on the front lines of the abortion debate, others on the protection of marriage from radical homosexuality. Still others will focus mainly on taxes or the gun rights issue. We all have a bit of knowledge of all the issues, or a lot of knowledge about a few. Most likely, we will be able to focus on the few and network with others on the larger number of issues.

So, pray and then take action on the issues the Lord lays on your heart. Be careful not to neglect the other issues, and please don't put up barriers between your issue and someone else's issue. This is one way the other side divides and conquers. Have you ever noticed how it seems like every antiliberty initiative has a huge number of left-wing activist nuts marching for it? Are there that many crazy people in this nation? The answer is no, there are not, but what the other side does well is build coalitions of the various crackpot organizations. You will often see the animal rights groups marching with the abortion advocates. Antigun organizers will march with antiwar groups. Pro-homosexual activists will march with animal rights activists. But rarely do we see the local gun rights group protesting the abortion clinic or standing hand in hand with pro-lifers in a march for life. Fiscal responsibility activists need to be marching with pro-marriage forces, and pro-lifers need to be working with those fighting amnesty for illegal aliens.

It is time we all got involved and worked with one another; there is strength in numbers, and that is something we have—and the other side only dreams of having. The average American is not a pro-abortion, animal-worshiping, tax-my-pants-off, antigun, homosexual activist. The truth is, the average American is much like they were in the 1700s. They want government to leave them alone; they respect life; they want to hold on to more of what they work so hard for; and they believe they have a right to defend themselves, their neighbors, and their liberties. We are indeed the majority, but we are an *all-too-silent* majority.

Now I realize time is precious for us all. Believe me, I understand this. I am constantly working from the early hours of the morning to the late hours of the night—and especially as I write this book. In addition to my other responsibilities, I need to see my family and be the spiritual leader for them. I need to add here that I do not see my family as separate from the battle we face politically. I encourage them to get involved as well, and my wife is a wonderful helpmeet in this area. She stays informed and is active on the issues. My wife is not likely to immediately engage you in political conversation—or at least, she wasn't likely to do so in former days—but I remember an occasion where I was preparing to press a legislator on a gun rights/personal defense issue. Before I could get the words out of my mouth, my wife had cornered the guy and was giving him "what for" on why she thought he was out of touch with reality. She made clear she expected his immediate attention to and support for pro-gun legislation. I just stood back and tried not to laugh, as she left him little room to consider anything but support of the bill. Sure enough, by the first of the next week that legislator had signed on as a cosponsor of the bill. Now I am sure he read the bill and realized its importance to liberty, but it took one of his constituents—my wife—to bring it to his attention and call for his immediate action. The adage attributed to Sir Edmund Burke, "All that is required for evil to prevail is for good men to do nothing," can be equally true if we reverse it. All it takes to overcome evil is for good men to act.

Ask for Wisdom

I have noted before that God is the giver of all wisdom, and that He is willing to freely give it to us if we simply ask. As believers, our votes and our political action need always to reflect God's wisdom.

In the election of Barack Obama, 96 percent of black Americans voted for him for president.[1] Now, I know without a shadow of a doubt that 96 percent of black Americans are *not* atheists. I know that a great number of blacks in the United States are self-proclaimed Christians and regularly attend church. Why, then, did so many of the black Christians vote for a candidate for public office who is adamantly opposed to God's expressed will?

By his words and his actions, Barack Hussein Obama Jr. is very clear about where he stands on certain issues. He is in favor of homosexuality. He not only has appointed more homosexuals to high government office than any previous president, but also he is openly pushing for open homosexuality in the military. He has appointed a militant, homosexual activist (his "safe schools" czar, Kevin Jennings) to oversee the indoctrination of our children with the particulars of this perverse lifestyle.

Barack Obama demonstrated that he is in favor of killing innocent babies in their mothers' wombs. As a state senator in Illinois, he voted *four times* to stop a bill that would mandate that medical personnel give life-saving treatment to an infant born alive after a botched abortion.[2] Essentially, if the abortionist failed to kill the child, then the proposed law would mandate that medical personnel help it live. Up to that point there were barbaric procedures that required a child born alive after a botched abortion be wrapped in a towel and thrown in with the dirty linens until it died. What an abominable practice for any civilized nation! Here was a politician—Barack Obama—who was so antilife that he was willing to let helpless infants suffer when they could have been be saved.

Barack Obama is patently opposed to Israel and God's chosen people. In an interview with Israel Army Radio, Hagai Ben Artzi, the brother of Netanyahu's wife, Sara, reportedly said, "It needs to be said clearly and simply: There is an anti-Semitic president in the U.S. It's not that Obama doesn't sympathize with [Mr. Netanyahu, prime minister of Israel]. He doesn't sympathize with the people of Israel."[3] Christians, on the other hand, are commanded to bless these chosen ones.

Obama and his administration believe in denying the individual the right to keep and bear arms in the defense of their most basic God-given rights. This can be seen in his hiring of Eric Holder as attorney general. Holder defended the D.C. Gun Ban of 2008. On the Web site OntheIssues.org, Obama's voting record and activities against guns are noted as a state senator and U.S. senator. He endorsed the Illinois Gun Ban of 2008, limiting gun purchases in September of 2007 and the ban of semi-automatic firearms and additional state gun restrictions in July 1998.[4]

In the face of all this evidence, how could any Christian of good conscience vote for this man to lead our nation? I can tell you. It's because the Christian voters who voted for Mr. Obama—black and white—allowed their emotions to get in the way of their convictions as to what is clearly right and wrong. The same can be said for the self-proclaimed evangelicals who voted for Bill Clinton *the second time*—after all of his shenanigans in the Oval Office and his support for much of the same agenda Obama is advancing!

My friend, judgment begins with the house of God. In order for us to really make a stand against the crisis our government is leading us into, our votes and our values had better line up with what God tells us in His Word, and the issues we advocate for had better match that same standard. God will hold us accountable.

Our emotions can get us into a lot of trouble. I know a large majority of black Christians voted for Obama. Some said it was simply because of his skin color—but is that really the excuse you are going to present to God if He asks why you voted for someone who is clearly in such opposition to Him? Many of us have voted for someone because we "felt" we liked them but had little knowledge of where they stood on the issues. Worse yet, how many have voted for someone in hopes of personal gain, knowing that they are really the wrong candidate?

We had better start getting on our knees and seeking God's wisdom on these matters! A lady called our radio show just after the race had ended between George W. Bush and then Vice President Al Gore. She called to repent for voting for Mr. Gore. She had learned after her vote that he was pro-abortion, and she recounted the story of how her mother had performed abortions and how she had to flush the babies down the toilet. This woman was in tears and absolutely distraught. She was also angry, as she had asked her pastor which candidate she should vote for; he unequivocally advised her to vote for Al Gore. When she became aware of Gore's stance, she confronted her pastor and asked him if he knew of Gore's view on the matter. The pastor responded that yes, he knew Gore's position.

Folks, this was a pastor who, because of greater loyalty to party than to his Creator, openly supported a candidate who opposed God's principles. When this woman rebuked the pastor for telling her to vote for Gore, his response was, "Then don't vote for him again." That guy is going to have a lot to answer for on the Day of Judgment!

This incident underscores the responsibility each of us has to study the issues and the candidates to make sure their records match their rhetoric. It also clearly demonstrates our responsibility to know as much as possible about the men we sit under each week in our churches. If we remain under such false teaching, then we too will be held accountable.

We have a responsibility to be salt and light, but we also are instructed in the parable of the talents to "occupy" until the Master returns. We are to be active and take dominion in every aspect of society. If you had a cure for cancer, would you withhold it from anyone—or would you try to treat everyone afflicted with this dreadful disease? Likewise, when you have wisdom from on high that is freely available to all, should we not employ that godly direction in order to protect the liberties that are a natural right of all men?

The answer is clear: we have a responsibility to ourselves, our nation, and to future generations to become active in politics. Some will say, "There is no hope," or "What is going to happen will happen." If that is what they really believe, then I offer them this challenge: Since we are all going to die eventually, why not just stop buying groceries and water and go ahead and die? Of course that is just as absurd as the notion that we sit on the sidelines when it comes to issues that affect our lives and our livelihoods and just let it happen to us. No, the marching orders are to occupy, and there is no wavering from that directive. We will not win all of the battles we take on, but if we do nothing, then we are just as responsible for the loss of liberty as those who are trying to take it.

Political Pharisees

On a final note, let me address something that has caused a lot of unnecessary conflict within the ranks of those fighting for liberty. It is the notion of "purity." Some have left one political organization or another because someone didn't do things exactly like they thought they should be done. This is the "I'm more pure than you" mentality that manifests itself in those who become "political Pharisees." This is largely to blame for the lack of coalition among those who love liberty. Thankfully that is beginning to change. It does our cause no good to be divided over the color of the church pews or who spends more time outside protesting. We all have something in common, and it is called liberty. With so many enemies of liberty, we have neither the time nor the energy to bicker with one another. This is not saying we will agree all of the time. Scripture is clear that we should discuss and at times debate the issues in what is called "iron sharpening iron." Discussing the issues makes us better at defending the issues, just as studying the Bible and discussing it with fellow believers makes us better students and more able to defend our beliefs.

My friends, liberty is given *by God*, but it must be defended *by us*. It is a gift worth protecting and defending. I used to call my grandfather almost every Veteran's Day to thank him for his service to liberty in World War II. One year he told me he appreciated the calls, but he thought he must not have done a good enough job because he had come to the conclusion that I would have to fight for liberty. I gave it some thought for a day or so and called him back to say that I would have to respectfully disagree with him. He had fought hard for liberty, received severe injuries, and had paved the way for the next generation. I told him that it was clear to me that *every generation* has the same responsibility. I thanked him for giving me that inheritance of liberty and told him that now it was my time to fight and pass on to the next generation the opportunity to protect and cherish the rich gift of liberty given to us all by God. He had not failed; quite the contrary. He had done his duty, and he continues to be active in voting and in other issues that affect his community. Until recently he even served on a local community board, giving of his time and wisdom for the benefit of his community.

Now it is our turn. Will we be the bearers and protectors of liberty for another generation? The choice is ours. The consequences— whether for good or ill—will be ours as well.

PART 3
RELIGION

CHAPTER 15

CHRISTIANS SHOULD NOT BE IGNORANT OR WIMPY

A Christian's Responsibility in These Perilous Times

By Chuck Bates

H OW MANY TIMES HAVE WE SEEN THE MEDIA IN RECENT years put down Christians as some sort of goofy fringe group? The number is probably countless. Almost every day we see another assault on a church, a ministry leader, or a "Christian" activist. The controlled media rarely miss an opportunity to put Christianity and its adherents in a bad light—essentially, acting as a casting director for public opinion and inferring that Christians are backward people and out of touch with reality. Christianity is treated as though it is the enemy of mankind—a virtual Taliban that should be avoided at all costs. In colleges and universities, our children are taught that to believe the stories in the Bible is arcane and old-fashioned. Unfortunately, many in the church who are self-proscribed "Christians" have begun to believe this big lie, and as a result they shy away from their own "beliefs." Even a number of well-known preachers and ministers have begun to water down the gospel and its power to make it more palatable to a society that is resistant to conviction regarding their thoughts, beliefs, and behavior. Tolerance is "in," and biblical truth is largely "out" in much of what masquerades as the church today.

But why—and how—did we get to this point? How did we go

from the fiery sermons of Jonathan Edwards, Charles Spurgeon, and Dwight Moody—or the clear gospel messages of Billy Graham and Billy Sunday—to the watered-down pabulum that is running like a river in the church today? Edwards's sermon "Sinners in the Hands of an Angry God" brought grown men to tears, with some literally running into the streets in repentance before God. Sadly, we no longer have among us such preachers as W. A. Criswell or Adrian Rogers, who stood on solid conviction and had more fear of God than they did of man. We have an entire generation growing up under the teachings of men who once may have had a clear direction from the Lord but seem willing now to sacrifice the obedience and satisfaction of preaching the Word of God for the seductions of fame and fortune. I dare say that we are at the precipice of losing an entire generation to such lackluster, namby-pamby "preaching." This is particularly true in the Western church.

In areas of the world where Christians face daily persecution, true believers must find it ludicrous to imagine "Christians" anywhere whose timid "faith" amounts to little more than a politically correct posture adopted to insure they won't offend anyone with their Jesus. As a matter of fact, Jesus said in Mark 8:38, "For whoever is ashamed of Me and My words in this adulterous and sinful generation, of him the Son of Man also will be ashamed when He comes in the glory of His Father with the holy angels." Pretty frightening when you think about it. Believers who face persecution rarely waste the time preaching prosperity doctrines, feel-good doctrines, or seeker-friendly doctrines. They haven't the inclination to waste the truth of God on the futile machinations of man. The state of the Christian church in the United States has become so dire that I have met missionaries from Africa who have been sent to the United States to preach the unadulterated gospel of Christ! How far the "church" has strayed today.

Consider the changes in many mainline denominations in this country over just the last twenty years. The Episcopal, Presbyterian,

Lutheran, and other denominations not only have accepted homo-sexuality as acceptable, but some have also gone so far as to ordain and place openly homosexual individuals in positions of high leadership and authority! Take, for example, Gene Robinson—a professed homosexual who left his wife and children for a man who was "enthroned" in 2004 as the Episcopal bishop for New Hampshire. Look at the Presbyterian Church (USA), where in 2008 they took up language for their church constitution that would rewrite previous versions, essentially opening the congregations to the acceptance of homosexuality among its members. Now, the Bible is very clear on the matter, and the condemnation of this abhorrent sexual behavior is outlined in both the Old and New Testaments. In the first chapter of Romans, Paul cites ungodly practices that, if the individual continues to practice them, will preclude one from entering heaven and receiving the rewards of salvation through Christ. The practice of homosexuality is on that list. It doesn't get much clearer. God's Word states:

> For the wrath of God is revealed from heaven against all ungodliness and unrighteousness of men, who suppress the truth in unrighteousness, because what may be known of God is manifest in them, for God has shown it to them....because, although they knew God, they did not glorify Him as God, nor were thankful, but became futile in their thoughts, and their foolish hearts were darkened. Professing to be wise, they became fools, and changed the glory of the incorruptible God into an image made like corruptible man....Therefore God also gave them up to uncleanness, in the lusts of their hearts, to dishonor their bodies among themselves, who exchanged the truth of God for the lie, and worshiped and served the creature rather than the Creator, who is blessed forever. Amen. For this reason God gave them up to vile passions. For even their women exchanged the natural use for what is against nature. Likewise also the men, leaving the natural use of

the woman, burned in their lust for one another, men with men committing what is shameful [homosexual acts], and receiving in themselves the penalty of their error which was due. *And even as they did not like to retain God in their knowledge,* God gave them over to a debased mind, to do those things which are not fitting; being filled with all unrighteousness, sexual immorality, wickedness, covetousness, maliciousness; full of envy, murder, strife, deceit, evil-mindedness; they are whisperers, backbiters, *haters of God*, violent, proud, boasters, inventors of evil things, disobedient to parents, undiscerning, untrustworthy, unloving, unforgiving, unmerciful; *who, knowing the righteous judgment of God, that those who practice such things are deserving of death, not only do the same but also approve of those who practice them.*

—Excerpts from Romans 1:18–32,
emphasis added

Despite a clear warning from Scripture, this week there will be another goofy lesson or a television advertisement by one of these "all-inclusive" groups that will put yet more doubt as to the reality of Christianity in the minds of the average viewer. Let me be perfectly clear: God loves the sinner and hates the sin. But, as noted in the verses from Romans, even God has a limit to His patience; He will not tolerate the most vile and open rebellion against His Word and truth.

You see, I am fully convinced, as every true believer in Jesus Christ should be, that if God said it, then that's that…end of story. We serve a mighty God—one who is also mighty patient, mighty loving, and mighty tolerant of our continued failure to appropriate His Word and will. He was willing to save Sodom and Gomorrah for ten righteous men, *but there were not even that many to be found.* The city had become so vile and evil that a crowd of wicked inhabitants pounded on Lot's door and demanded he send out his visitors—angels sent by God to rescue Lot and his family—so they could rape them. Depravity of that degree is hard for most of us to imagine, but wicked deeds of that magnitude take place daily in our nation and have even crept into many institutions that call themselves churches across the country. I heard a famous preacher once say something to the effect that, "If you think God is in favor of homosexuality, then let me refer you to His urban renewal program for Sodom and Gomorrah!"

God does not lie, my friends. His Word is very clear about how we should live our lives. None of us are without sin, but Romans 1 describes a point where individuals knew they were openly sinning and yet they continued to mock God, rejoicing in what was their eternal death sentence. It is terrible to even ponder the wickedness that must reside in hearts so rebellious that a loving and compassionate God would finally sear their consciences and turn away from them, abandoning them to their unnatural practices.

As bad as that is, how much different is it when a church decides to kick against biblical precepts, embracing the sinner and the sin with open arms, not only failing to admonish them but encouraging the very thing God says is despicable and evil? How long will God be patient with us?

Too Much Emotion and Too Little Thought

How did we get to this point? Simply put, it comes from too much emotion and too little thought. Don't get me wrong; God created our emotions for a reason. He created our desire for our spouse, He created our anger over injustices, and He created our joy in worshiping Him. But nowhere do I see in His Word that He desires that we be ruled or led solely by emotion. God has given us marvelous faculties to do His will on the earth. And while our emotions are indeed an integral part of our being, we rarely are served by allowing them to rule our lives. Just observe your teenagers who are often run by their emotions, constantly tossed to and fro by the latest impulse. If you have small children, observe the irrational temper tantrums they throw when they don't get their way. Mature believers should not indulge in such childish ways. Unfortunately, many in the church act like spiritual babies, never growing but remaining in a perpetual state of the "spiritual newborn," craving milk rather than the meat of spiritual truth. The apostle Paul addresses this in 1 Corinthians 3:1–3: "And I, brethren, could not speak to you as to spiritual people but as to carnal, as to babes in Christ. I fed you with milk and not with solid food; for until now you were not able to receive it, and even now you are still not able; for you are still carnal. For where there are envy, strife, and divisions among you, are you not carnal and behaving like mere men?"

We are supposed to be growing up in our faith and moving from glory to glory as we press into the truth of the Word of God. But how can that happen if believers are being led astray by their emotions? There are pastors who have tapped into the spiritual immaturity and lusts of the congregations they lead and have captured entire audiences with fun-sounding doctrines that promise everything from a life free of problems to a sort of "spiritual lottery," where everyone is entitled to a mansion, a Rolls-Royce, and a garage to park it in! This is a rising trend in many of our local communities. Not three miles from my office sits a church that has almost exclusively preyed on the emotions of gullible, spiritual babes, and the result is a spiritually retarded congregation.

When I see a preacher riding in a chauffeured limousine to "his" church, where he will work his congregation into such a frenzy of giving that they give the rent money to the preacher instead of the landlord, something is seriously wrong. These people are being driven by overriding emotion.

Getting It Right

The intent of this book is not to name the failures and false doctrines of big-name preachers or televangelists; rather, it is to awaken the church to get back to basic biblical principles and responsibilities so that we can be a light in these critical days as the world around us gropes in the dark for answers to its crises. The body of Christ—which includes pastors, teachers, and all the rest of us—has a serious responsibility for the furthering of the gospel.

Responsibility number one is to get right with God and to seek His will, His ways, and His wisdom for our lives. Second, if you are the head of your household, you are to be the spiritual leader of your family. Additionally we all have a responsibility to grow in our faith and relationship with Christ.

If my wife and I were still at the relational level we had while dating, we would be doing something wrong. Instead, as the years pass, we continue to grow in our relationship, leaving the childish things behind and moving to a higher level of relationship as we utilize the wisdom and experiences we have gained. The same is true in our walk with God. We are to be spiritual meat eaters, not babies in the church nursery. Pastors, in turn, have all of the above responsibilities but with the added burden of "getting it right" as they teach their congregations. The Word cautions all of us in this regard: "My brethren, let not many of you become teachers, knowing that we shall receive a stricter judgment" (James 3:1).

The congregations have a responsibility to rightly divide the Word as well, because ultimately it is a personal relationship with Christ, not a surrogate relationship through a pastor or minister. Philippians 2:12–13 instructs the believer, "Therefore, my beloved, as you have always obeyed, not as in my presence only, but now much more in my absence, work out your own salvation with fear and trembling; for it is God who works in you both to will and to do for His good pleasure." Paul was telling the church that it was time they left the spiritual nest to walk on their own as they seek God and His will. He was replicating himself and the Word in the people so they would be equipped to disciple others. This is what the Christian life is to be about, not "sitting close to the spout where the glory comes out," hoping to win the heavenly lotto. Sitting in a pew, waiting on someone to feed you the same milk week after week will render you practically useless for the kingdom.

We have to grow up as a church. The Western institution that calls itself the church is by and large failing. It is failing to realize and practice basic biblical principles. Its people are failing to develop and utilize spiritual muscle, failing to challenge one another and to hold one another accountable in their walk. The Western church has become lazy, and this, my friend, is manifest disobedience. Is this sin against God any less egregious than the sin of practicing homosexuality?

Pastors, you need to wake up to the world around you; lead your flock to become relevant to the society around them. Stop seeking answers from the world; instead, become the answer center for the world.

Less than two hundred years ago, the church was the center for wisdom in commerce, religion, art, literature, and even politics. However, as the church began to turn away from the responsibility of educating the world on what God had to say in all of these matters, it became, by degrees, irrelevant.

In the last one hundred years, the church has abdicated its responsibility for the welfare of the poor, the widows, and the orphans. Instead, it has allowed a godless government to take over that responsibility. Instead of giving folks the temporary help they need and then encouraging them to get back on their feet and care for their families, we have allowed secular humanists to come in and disrupt God's order. With many living on the "government plantation," fathers have been kicked out of the home and have become largely irrelevant. This is a wrong that must be corrected NOW!

I recently had the pleasure of interviewing Pastor Eric Bahme from Portland, Oregon, on our nationally syndicated radio program. His book, *The MBE Revolution*, is a must-read for any pastor or ministry leader looking to get back to the practical ministry of the gospel. In a nutshell, the church Eric Bahme pastors set up a business and purchased two run-down motels in a drug-and-prostitution-infested area near Portland. They use this for-profit hospitality (hotel) business to reach people with the gospel of Jesus Christ.

As a result of their efforts, they have been able to minister to real people with real hurts in need of real wisdom and direction in their lives. Over the last few years they have seen over two thousand travelers to their hotels come to profess Christ as their personal Savior! In the process, they have made money that has subsequently been used to fund a recovery program for drug abusers and alcoholics, the largest family homeless shelter in the nation ($3.5 million and not a dime of government money), a job training program, and much more—*all to the glory of God*. They have developed an economic model that not only impacts the community but also helps fund the ministry.

Additionally just six months after taking over the properties that had become havens for prostitution and meth production, they received a letter from the Portland Police Department, thanking them for their efforts and acknowledging that the church had accomplished—in just a few short months—a reduction in crime and a change in the community that the government had been unable to do in ten years!

Friends, that is real and relevant Christianity. An unexpected benefit is that the for-profit model allows the congregation to get involved in political issues affecting the family and the community that otherwise would be off limits for nonprofit 501c(3) organizations.

Don't Be Afraid to Get Involved

I have been involved in politics from the local level here in Tennessee to the White House, having worked in the George H. W. Bush administration, and I can say without hesitation that church politics can be more vicious than anything in the world, so let's all get over our fears and reservations and get our churches active in the public forum. We have a responsibility to bring to our society the wisdom of God Almighty, and in order to do so, we have to quit hiding behind our church walls. This hiding contributes to the perception that Christians are wimps and out of touch because we often fail to get involved in the very things that affect our daily lives. Pastors, you need to know what the wolves of the world look like so you can better educate and train your congregations. Don't fear stepping on a few toes as you tell the truth. Believe me—those who are serious about their walk with the Lord will thank you.

I have been in a number of churches in my travels over the years. I have served on the board of a local church, and currently my wife and our family attend a church that is very serious about teaching the Bible as the inspired, infallible, and inerrant Word of God, and I can be pretty cynical when it comes to preachers and pabulum. I assure you, I am not alone in this line of thought. You may not realize just how many in the congregation are ready to cry out and demand that you tell the truth and challenge the church to get up and get with it.

Because of the tentative and uncertain message coming from many of our nation's pulpits, spiritual men are increasingly skeptical about the institution that masquerades as God's church. You would be amazed at the many spiritual warriors waiting for the leaders of churches to take a stand on the truths of God. So why are they not standing themselves? Simply put, many are in a quandary as to where they can be challenged and grow in their walk with the Lord in a body of believers that take it as seriously as they do.

We have witnessed an emotional threat over the last twenty to thirty years that has paralyzed the institution of the church to the point of irrelevance; it is called *fear*. Much of the church has more fear of man than fear of God. This is the root of much of the problem in the church today, both in the United States and in other nations. We have decided that our concerns over what man may think of us outweigh our responsibility to God and to our congregations as preachers of the truth. We fail to do right, and we risk the consequence of becoming that "sinner in the hands of an angry God." Let me tell you—that is far more frightening than what any man could ever dream of doing to you!

There are times when I realize the pastor of the church I attend is forced to preach milk again and again for those who won't take up their spiritual responsibilities. It grieves my spirit. There are many reading this book who understand exactly what I am writing here. You too have a yearning for the church to get with it and grow up.

Help your fellow believers in this endeavor. Allow God to lead you into their lives to disciple them; in the process you will grow as well. Encourage the pastors where you fellowship to challenge the congregation to grow up spiritually. Be there when that preacher needs an armor bearer or simply another mature believer to talk with.

Pastors, don't limit those in your congregation who are ready to "kick it up a notch" for the kingdom. They will be of immense help to you as the congregation moves on to that next phase in God's will and as you begin to see a greater impact on your local community.

Church, it is time we quit being an easy target for the world to kick around. It is time for the world to take notice of the people of God. God has given us an instruction manual called the Bible. He has given us the answers for a world crying out for answers. We are not called to conform to the world; rather, we are called to help the world conform to God. In the process, we further the kingdom of God. We cooperate with His purpose to reconcile His creation and His people back unto Himself. We can be the people that the world seeks out to help answer their questions, whether temporal or eternal. Our members should be affecting every area of our world as salt and light. Salt is a preservative and an antiseptic, but it must be next to the patient's wound to be of any use.

The church has all the wisdom and direction man needs. The "catch" is that we—the body of Christ—must first be willing to appropriate it in our own lives. We must grow up and use the marvelous talents, abilities, and faculties our Creator has given us to do His will on Earth. Further, it requires us to seek His wisdom and discernment daily. Pastors, some of you may be stinging from what we have discussed in this chapter, but let me ask you to lay aside all pride and sincerely ask God to reveal to you His will in your life and the direction of the ministry that you lead.

We must be obedient, get back to the basics, do God's will, and risk the consequences. In the end the only one we really have to answer to is God Himself. Our communities, our nation, and our world needs us. Will you take the challenge?

CHAPTER 16

WHAT HAPPENED TO THE FATHERS?

Restoring Order in a Fatherless Generation

By Larry Bates and Chuck Bates

T HERE IS NO ARGUMENT THAT SOCIETY AS A WHOLE FACES a lot of problems. But whether the problem is financial, political, or even issues in the realm of religion, they all boil down to one common denominator: man's sin nature and rebellion against God's order for His creation. There is a natural order that, when followed, allows all things to flow relatively smoothly. I am not suggesting we will ever be able to have a man-made utopia; that is impossible outside of the return of Christ. However, we can certainly avoid a lot of life's obstacles if we are willing to be obedient to God's divine order.

When you look at a clock or the inside of an old watch, you will see wheels, gears, and crystals that comprise a mechanism designed to work in perfect order and keep time as accurately as possible. With the elements in proper order, the watch will work according to the designer's plan, but each gear and each cog must be in proper order for the watch or clock to run at all. It is a type of man imitating God. We could examine a variety of such examples: car engines and helicopters, things in nature such as the life cycle of predator and prey, and the oceans being fed by the rivers, which are fed by the rains coming from clouds that draw their moisture from the oceans. It all points to God's master plan for humanity.

God has an order for society as a whole, and it is very simple: God over man, man over woman, man and woman over children. (See Ephesians 5:23.) This is God's order for the family. Very simple. Unfortunately, this has become the exception rather than the rule in our society. We cannot afford to be in rebellion against God concerning this. Scripture is clear on what rebellion leads to. First Samuel 15:23 says, "Rebellion is as the sin of witchcraft" (KJV).

Contrary to what you may have heard from some seeker-friendly preacher not grounded in the Word of God, we all have sinned and fallen short of His glory. Yes, we all have a sin nature. If it were not for sin, we would have had no need for a Savior.

I am reminded of a Sunday school class my dad was teaching years ago; the issue of our sin nature and our rebellion against God came up as the topic of study one week. A lady in the class boldly said her children did not sin, as they were children. My dad made an equally clear point that *we all sin* and asked what would happen if you put a couple of two-year-olds in a room with one toy. Well, anyone who has children knows the answer: the sin nature that each child was born with will manifest. Both of them will want the toy, and the battle for the toy will begin. Sin is something we all have to deal with, but we can live in everlasting gratitude that God was gracious enough to give us an order of living that can help us avoid many of life's pitfalls.

The Disordered Household Epidemic

We need to go back to a place where biblical order can be established in our families. The media constantly bombard us with images of women being in control over their husbands, their households, and in the workplace. From cartoons to commercials to comedy series, men and women are not shown to respect and love each other the way God intended. Wives are portrayed as hard, cold, and driven, often making fun of husbands who are shown to be couch potatoes, undereducated, and lazy.

This is contrary to the true intention God had in mind for the family where women respect, encourage, and support their husbands, and men love their wives as Christ loved the church by being her spiritual leader, protector, and provider.

Generations of women have been wrongly taught that they are supposed to be in control and liberated from the bonds imposed by men—while generations of men have been taught by their fathers' examples that they should fly under the radar, not cause too many waves, and let their wives do all the hard stuff of managing the household, disciplining the children, and calling the family together for devotions. It seems that too many men and women are so far detached from God's ideal that we are seeing disrupted homes, destroyed marriages, and disillusioned children.

There is a lot of talk of the "Jezebel spirit" in churches today. But in order for a Jezebel to exist, there must also be an Ahab who allows it to happen. You may remember the account in the Bible of Ahab and Jezebel. Ahab was such a wimp and a pushover that he actually enabled the sin of an out-of-control household. By not exercising his proper role, Ahab was responsible for great losses, including lives, and there was in that nation nearly a generation held in bondage by worship of false gods.

Thankfully, God sent a warrior to "right the ship," so to speak, and bring order back to the land. Unfortunately for Jezebel, she did not willingly submit to God's order, and she met a very nasty fate. Ahab died even before Jezebel; he was fleeing an enemy that God certainly could have routed, but because of his disobedience to God he died at the hands of his enemies. His sons followed in his footsteps and met similar fates.

This was a house that was out of order, and its dysfunction impacted a nation. How did Ahab get to this point? He rebelled against God's order from the very start by marrying a woman out of political expediency and gain. Jezebel was not just any woman but a pagan who took her false religion seriously—to the point of fanaticism. Had Ahab adhered to God's direction, he would have never married Jezebel, as Scripture was clear in its warnings about such situations. Alas, this man's sin nature overtook him, and as a result, Ahab was the most wicked king of Israel up to that time.

This same scenario is playing out in households across this nation. The results of the "disordered household epidemic" have led us down a path of some unintended consequences:

1. Children losing respect for both dad and mom, and in turn developing a skewed understanding of God as their Father. Their entire worldview of the roles set up by God is turned upside down, and the problem of living outside God's intended order is perpetuated for the next generation because the current generation has not had good role models.

2. High rates of divorce for reasons other than what God gave us allowance for because of the hardness of our hearts. Neither men nor women understand anymore what it means to put in the hard work it takes to have a successful godly marriage. Our children are not able to see us allow God to soften our hearts so that we can be the husband or wife He wants us to be. We give up when it gets too hard. We take on the victim role and feel entitled to a certain kind of treatment from our spouse, and if we don't get it the marriage ends. This kind of thinking is what adds to the vast majority of divorce cases in the nation that are filed as "no-fault." This is an utter shame.

3. Single parenthood and out-of-wedlock births are
on the rise because we can't seem to surrender to
what God's plan is for relationships. We'd rather do
it on our own than do it God's way, but we have to
remember who the real victims are—our children.

I realize that every situation has its own nuances, but if we are really honest, it ultimately gets down to our submission to God's authority and His order for our lives. What has blurred our vision toward God's order for our lives? Do we pay more attention to the popular culture than to God's order? I think the answer is obvious. This must stop if we are to restore the family and in turn restore our nation.

Government-Promoted Fatherlessness

The godly model of what a family should be is being attacked from all sides. Even the government has had a hand in creating disorder in the American household. From nonsensical and intrusive agencies to specifically targeted segments of society set up for failure, we have seen how a godless government can do little real good but a lot of real damage by getting families out of God's perfect order. One of the places where I see this most is the welfare system. Segments of our society are targeted by this system in what amounts to social engineering and a kind of bondage that sows perpetual disorder in the lives of millions of Americans. Let's face it—Satan wants to steal, kill, and destroy, and the family is his number one target because it is the foundation of any society.

It is absurd to think that any entity can successfully replace God as head of the family, but that's just what our government tries to do. Unfortunately the proof for this can be seen in the way liberal politicians have courted African American families for the last five decades.

As was mentioned before in chapter 1, empty promises have

been made to African American families by liberal politicians seeking votes to get into office. They make these vain promises to pass legislation that would seem to end all of their economic and social ills, but the liberals have not kept their promise. The evidence for this is overwhelming.

Robert Kessler reported in his book *Inside the White House* that the late 1960s President Lyndon Johnson, a Democrat, sought to pass "civil rights" legislation so sweeping in its nature that he was noted to have said, "I'll have [derogatory term for black people] voting Democrat for the next two hundred years."[1]

While the concept of government assistance during hard economic times didn't begin with Johnson, his promise to pull black Americans out of poverty with the Great Society plan would cause a majority of them to wholeheartedly support Democratic candidates. His party has experienced almost unanimous support from the vast majority of blacks in America. But the lure of government help and assistance to live life free from ghettos, poor health care and education, and crime proved to be nothing more than rhetoric.

Back in the 1970s when he was a Tennessee legislator, my dad had to deal with this stark reality. It seemed that in order to fully gain from the system, families were encouraged to split up. The system was set up to make it easier to obtain if the family's household income is below a certain threshold. With a father in the house (husband or not), household income levels rise (usually just above the cut-off), and the benefits are not approved for that family. So what's easier? Get a second job and live within your means, or let the father move out and get government assistance?

In addition, the more children one had, the more money the government would "give" them—provided there was not a father in the house. The result, in some cases, was that laziness, out-of-wedlock births, and a general abdication of God's order got many people government rewards. But if a person remained married and walked by God's laws, they were penalized—and so it is today, as evidenced by the fact that married people are taxed higher than those who just "shack up."

Let me just say this, the welfare system and other government programs like it that intervene in family affairs have affected families across all ethnicities. Also, there are black families who are successfully following God's plan for the family and are working hard to educate future generations about how to live in godly order, but the numbers on this don't lie.

Prior to the Great Society legislation signed by Johnson, black communities and businesses were growing, and poverty among blacks was falling quickly. Harlem, for example, was a bustling center of economic activity. Black businessmen had their own insurance companies, banks, universities, theaters, retail establishments, factories, and so on. Poverty among black Americans dropped nearly 17 percent from 1960 to 1970.[2] But just a few years after the Great Society took hold, those numbers came to a standstill, and the economic well-being of families in black communities began to slide as well. Prior to Johnson's "secure the black vote" plan, very few black babies were born out of wedlock. Today, over 70 percent of black babies are born out of wedlock.[3] This is a travesty!

As I said before, it's not just the black family that has suffered under LBJ's Great Society largesse. These statistics are becoming a reality in white and Hispanic communities as well—and they all have a common denominator: God's order for the family has been replaced with man's rebellious order. Despite the pervasiveness of this rebellion, it is killing the black community faster than any other sector of our society. We have to wake up to this reality and put a stop to it.

A Description of Godly Family Order

Men, this is where we talk responsibility. If you were not raised with the proper order in your house, then by all means find some men in your church who were and have them mentor you in this area. Godly mentoring will give you a new freedom and boldness to obey God, and it will aid you in bringing order to your home. Ultimately, this is what is needed to restore our nation.

As the head of our households, we carry a huge responsibility for our families before God. We are to be the spiritual as well as the physical head of the home. This does not give us *carte blanche* to act like a bunch of ogres, ruling like iron-fisted dictators. It does require us to be on our knees daily, seeking God's direction for our own lives and the lives of our wives and children. I have news for you, buddy: when you go before God, He is not going to ask how your preacher or your church did with teaching your kids about Him; it's all going to be on your shoulders!

Wives also play a critical supporting role that is of tremendous significance. My wife is of great value to me as the helpmeet God designed her to be. We discuss matters, and I seek my wife's input on major decisions in our family. At times she may see something that I don't, and certainly she is the more compassionate of the two of us. Together we make a great team, but I still have the responsibility to be head of our home and to discern where God would have us go in His greater purpose for our lives.

My wife is a "Proverbs 31 woman," and each year we are married I see how God stretches her to become even more of a blessing in that role. I encourage her to take steps of faith into new avenues such as teaching and mentoring. The Bible says that the older women should teach the younger women how to love their husbands and their children to take care of their home. (See Titus 2:3–5.) I see her doing this, and she continues to grow in the Lord as I do, and together we model this example to our daughter so she will grow up understanding the importance of God's order in her home.

Before you conclude that I must live in some kind of dreamland, let me clearly state that my wife and I are as human as anyone else. We have those "intense moments of fellowship" (otherwise known as disagreements), but we both know that God's order is for a divine purpose. My wife does not want to be the head; she knows it is out of order, and she realizes the weight of the responsibility I bear as head of our household.

For those who are not married yet and are looking for a godly mate, let me assure you that despite how screwed up our society is today, there are still people who know and desire God's order in their lives.

My wife and I got married a little later in life than is the norm, and I think both of us had pretty much come to the conclusion that it was nearly impossible to find a marriage partner who understood the proper order of things. I used to tell my dad that I thought perhaps I would have to be like Paul and not marry. I didn't think there were any truly godly women left in the world. Well, of course that upset him, as he wanted grandchildren, so he began praying for God to do a quick work. And boy—did He ever! The rest is history. I met the woman who was to be my wife not long after my dad started praying about it. We discussed the role of the husband and wife while we were dating and found ourselves to be in agreement on the matter of God's order. As a married couple, we have had it confirmed in our lives that when we do things according to God's way, life is just a whole lot smoother. He only puts His stamp of approval on us when we do things His way. The blessings of an intact, God-ordered family are innumerable.

Dr. Walter Williams—in my estimation, one of the greatest thinkers and economists of our day—has outlined a surefire way to live in poverty. In a nutshell, Dr. Williams said that if you want to live in poverty, then have sex outside of marriage, get pregnant or get someone pregnant, and then drop out of school to take care of the child. You will likely not marry, and the minimum-wage job that you likely will qualify for will not meet the bills, and you can then apply for government assistance. Your child(ren) can grow up in a system that, more often than not, will keep them in the same cycle for another generation.[4]

Now conversely, those who are least likely to end up destitute and on welfare will finish high school or college, get their finances in order (go to work), then get married to someone they love before they begin having children. Seems practical enough, and until about forty years ago that was the norm. Today, it is quickly becoming the exception to the rule. As a matter of fact, the local paper stopped printing all of the birth announcements because it was embarrassing to see all the out-of-wedlock births. I counted them each week, and almost without fail, nearly 50 percent of the children born in this area were born out of wedlock. That is definitely not in God's order.

Where Churches Are Failing

Just as God created an order for the household—God over man, man over woman, and man and woman over children—this same hierarchy should prevail in our local churches. There is much debate in Christian publications with regard to a woman's role in the church. The Scripture does not mince words on this topic. *The top leadership of any church must be made up of men.* Ephesians 5:22–27 clearly identifies God's order in the family, and the family does not stop at the end of your driveway; it extends to all aspects of life.

> Wives, submit to your own husbands, as to the Lord. For the husband is the head of the wife, as also Christ is head of the church; and He is the Savior of the body. Therefore, just as the church is subject to Christ, so let the wives be to their own husbands in *everything*. Husbands, love your wives, just as Christ also loved the church and gave Himself for her, that He might sanctify and cleanse her with the washing of water by the word, that He might present her to Himself

a glorious church, not having spot or wrinkle or any such
thing, but that she should be holy and without blemish.

—EMPHASIS ADDED

If that was not clear enough, we are instructed in 1 Timothy
chapters 2 and 3 that men are to lead the church body and that
women are expressly prohibited from teaching or having authority
over the men of the church. Chapter 3 demonstrates that a leader of
the church must be the husband of one wife. Clearly this indicates
the leadership of the early church was exclusively men. The problem
is that very few of our churches are making a stand on this.

The late W. A. Criswell was asked on a national television
show about his beliefs on women in the pulpit. He clearly stated,
somewhat tongue-in-cheek, that as soon as a woman could be the
husband of one wife his denomination would start making them
preachers. Does this mean that women have no place or function
in the church? Absolutely not! Women have a great role to play in
our local churches, but the order of leadership is not any different
from the family structure. Why would it be? Why would God be so
specific on the leadership in the home and on the husband as priest
of that home and then change the order when it came to church?
He wouldn't, and His Word indicates just that. I know the arguments that seek an explanation for leadership on the part of some
of the great women of the Bible, but in each of those cases—Esther,
Ruth, or Deborah, to name a few—each submitted to God's order
in their lives and were blessed for it.

I believe it is in God's order for women to teach other women
and children, but for women to have authority over the men in a
congregation is improper. Let's refer back to the responsibility given
to men as husbands and then look at the even greater responsibility
in the church setting.

The Bible makes clear that not many should seek to be teachers
or pastors, as they will be held to higher account at the judgment.
There are a number of parachurch ministries led by women, some

of them designed specifically to mentor women. But there are also a great number that are out of order, and many of the men who sit under them are out of order. The men are merely doing the same thing at church that they do at home, and that is let the women take the responsibility because they themselves are too lazy or rebellious to accept the leadership role.

Likewise, there are men in pulpits each week who are afraid of offending the women in the congregation with anything like what I am discussing. As a result, they would be hard-pressed to find any real men in their churches. *This is key.* It is one of the reasons that many Christian men avoid church like the plague: they cannot stomach the wimpy, effeminate pastors and preaching that ultimately result when women are given leadership over men in the church!

If you are one of the men in the pulpit who has more fear of men and women than you do God, then I suggest you either resign your position or repent and get right in God's order. Without a true shepherd, the sheep will scatter. Pastors need to take a close look at the direction and warnings in Ezekiel 34 and 35 with regard to their ultimate roles and responsibility. If you do not offer real answers from the Word, then you might as well run episodes of *Dr. Phil* each Sunday. But if you want to fulfill that role as a true pastor, then *sound a certain trumpet* so that the people will know the direction of the enemy and be prepared for the battle!

Folks, this is the truth, and not because I have put it to paper but because God said it first. There is not much in this world that makes me angrier than to sit in a church that is out of God's divine order. You might as well be shouting at the wall because that is as far as most of the preaching in that place will ever get. Lives are not changed, pastor, when you hold back on the truth of God from the pulpit. Women have a huge role in churches and ministries that are properly ordered.

Let me offer a final warning to the men. Even if your family and you are blessed to be sitting under the teaching of a real pastor, remember that ultimately the spiritual well-being and training of your family is your personal responsibility.

And wives, your place of importance in the lives of your children, and even more importantly as a help to your husband as he strives to accomplish the work before him, is absolutely essential. You should never take it lightly. May the Lord give us all wisdom in these uncertain days as we strive to run the race and fight the good fight of faith.

Prophetic Significance of Following God's Order

In Malachi 4:5–6 we read, "Behold, I will send you Elijah the prophet before the coming of the great and dreadful day of the LORD. And He will turn the hearts of the fathers to the children, and the hearts of the children to their fathers, lest I come and strike the earth with a curse."

I believe it is significant to point out that throughout Scripture, curses were primarily referenced when some king or people had done something to Israel. In Obadiah 15 we read, "For the day of the LORD upon all the nations is near; as you have done [to Israel], it shall be done to you; your reprisal shall return upon your own head." As we see world organizations and even our own government come against Israel, we cannot discount or escape the significance of God's warning.

We can clearly see God's order as He established the fathers of our faith—Abraham, Isaac, and Jacob—and their descendants. This brings us to the overview of two kingdoms at war, the kingdom of Satan challenging the kingdom of God. This brings us to our part in this war. All of our families and relationships have been and are being attacked. How well we understand God's historical family order (Abraham, Isaac, Jacob, and their descendants), as well as present-day application, will in large part determine how well we fare individually and as a nation.

The restoration of God's ultimate order will culminate in all that we read in the entire chapter of Romans 9 and Ephesians chapter 2. That is where Jew and Gentile alike become one new man, where both (Jew and Gentile) truly know their Messiah and experience God's order for all mankind. In Genesis 12:3, God had a specific promise to Abraham when He said, "I will bless those who bless you, and I will curse him who curses you; and in you all the families of the earth shall be blessed."

How the Church Can Fill the Gap

The fatherless generation needs someone to lead them into the proper order. It can't be left to the gangs and false religions that have been there to capitalize on this widespread dysfunction. We, the church and Christian families who are intact from all ethnic backgrounds, have responsibility. We have to be willing to look in the mirror and take responsibility for obeying God's order for the family. We can't sit around and just blame others for their problems—that's too easy.

The church needs to rise up and begin to teach that having children out of wedlock and sex before marriage is not in God's order. This next generation is getting so many mixed messages about sexual responsibility, about working hard, finishing a quality education, providing for a family, and being an influence to those around them, but we have all the answers. There may be a void of fathers in the world, but our churches need to be havens for the fatherless, a place where they can be trained up and mentored, where young men can be retaught what it means to have a father and a man of integrity in their lives, where young women know what it means to be wives, mothers, and mentors for future generations. This will give them the edge they need to thrive in the midst of the crisis we see our nation facing every day. We can arm our young people so that they won't be lazy and depend on the government, but they will know who their heavenly Father is and depend on His wisdom for the direction in which their lives should go.

We have a responsibility to model God's order in our homes and churches. Too much is at stake if we don't. I can assure you that when we do, all the gears and the cogs fit in place, and we can be truly effective for the kingdom of God and for our society.

Remember: judgment starts in the house of God, and Christ is coming for a bride without spot or wrinkle. There is a lot of work to do just getting God's order back in place in the institution that is supposedly representing Him on Earth.

Tony Evans once preached, "If you want to know what is wrong with a nation, I will take you to the states; and if you want to know what is wrong with the states, I will take you to the cities; if you want to know what is wrong in the cities, I take you to the local communities; and if you want to know what is wrong in the communities, I take you to the family!"[5]

It all starts at home, where we must first learn to practice God's order and restore men to their role as fathers and priests of their families. Equally, wives must take their position beside their husbands, together leading their children in the fear and admonition of the Lord. Will we always agree? Probably not. But obedience is the command, and the results are the blessings and protection of God. When we are obedient to these most basic things, God will continue to reveal Himself to us in greater dimensions. Once we have this spiritual framework and foundation in place, then we can truly be used to right the ship of society. This is the only way to bring order to the chaos that affects us in almost every way—financially, politically, and spiritually.

CHAPTER 17

THE BATTLE FOR YOUR CHILD'S MIND AND SOUL

How Christians Should Respond to the Secularizing of Education

By Chuck Bates

ALL OF US WANT OUR CHILDREN TO HAVE THE BEST OPPORtunities available to them. Our desire is that they get a good education in order to better themselves and the society around them, but are we getting what we pay for at the college level? Could we actually be endangering our children by sending them to college?

Let's be clear: I am very much in favor of education. My mother and my grandfather were educators, and my dad, Larry Bates, has taught money and banking courses in the college system and is a past president of the University of Tennessee National Alumni Association. That said, I want to emphasize that I am even more oriented toward performance. If the institution is not getting the job done, then it is not a place I want to send my children. Larry and I both have postgraduate degrees, and we are certainly not against higher education. However, far too many parents are entrusting their children to systems that do little to prepare them for the real job market. In fact, some institutions can mentally and spiritually damage them if we are not vigilant as parents, preparing them for the world at a young age then reinforcing that with prayer and support when they leave the nest.

History of Higher Education in America

Let's look at a little of the history of American higher education. In the 1700s the average entrant to any number of colleges would have been in their mid-teens and extremely literate. Long before any form of SAT or ACT entrance exam existed, most colleges not only would have expected their students to have a command of the English language but in addition, the student would likely know Latin and Greek and be well versed in literature that some college students today never hear of, much less read and recite.

Many of the institutions of the 1700s—Harvard College for one—were primarily turning out very literate preachers of the gospel to fill the church pulpits of the colonies. As a matter of fact, Harvard's earliest school motto was *Veritas Christo et Ecclesiae*, which translated literally means "Truth for Christ and the church." I dare say Harvard has come a long way from those roots, and you would be hard-pressed to find any semblance of such character in its classrooms today. Yet, despite the complete turnaround in Christian ideology, Harvard is treated as the *crème de la crème* of higher education. The mere mention of a Harvard education is supposed to open all doors in the workforce for the owner of such a prized diploma, and scads of money are expected to fall from the sky on all who claim Harvard as their alma mater.

This is not necessarily the reality, though. Many Harvard grads have indeed done well for themselves post college, while others have done little with their educations. The one thing they all have in common is that they likely spent huge sums of money for an education that may or may not be superior to any other college degree. It just cost a whole lot more than a degree from a local or state college down the road.

So why do we do it? Why do we scrape and even borrow to send our children to some of these institutions of "higher learning" if they are not all they are cracked up to be? I believe that sometimes it is because, as in so many other areas in our lives, some of us are trying to keep up with the Joneses or the Smiths. I have news for you, friend: the Joneses are trying to keep up with the Smiths, who are trying to keep up with the Robertses, who could care less about the other two. Many times it can be vain imaginations. What is *not* a vain imagination—*and is all too real*—is the damage that can potentially be heaped on the student and society from what passes for an education. I am not just picking on Harvard; many colleges and universities across the nation are putting some parents in hock while, through their liberal teachings, indoctrinating our kids.

College Is Not for Everyone

Recently, Larry had the opportunity to speak with the former president of the University of Tennessee, his alma mater. What he learned was shocking and disappointing. It turns out that in some schools, the K–12 education that we all pay for via our tax dollars is not adequately preparing our youth for college. The gentleman indicated that the university was spending millions of dollars annually in remedial education—just to bring their students up to speed on the basics for college-level work! Remedial English and math were at the top of the list. Adding to this burden has been the onslaught of students who previously have not entertained the idea of a college education but due to a perceived "need" for everyone to go, and the recent thinking that it is a "right" for all to go to college, institutions are seeing an influx of students who simply are not ready and in all honesty probably shouldn't be there in the first place.

We need to face the fact that not everyone is cut out for college. Not everyone is going to be a doctor, engineer, or lawyer. Some of our friends and family are not going to attain to those levels, either by choice or because they do not have the ability. Unfortunately, in an attempt to protect self-esteem, we have put people into positions they are not qualified to hold. There is no clearer representation of this than in the education establishment itself. The teachers' unions, such as the National Education Association (NEA) and the state organizations along with a number of higher education groups, have effectively insulated their members from competition in the marketplace of ideas. Take the public school districts of Chicago, Memphis, DC, and Detroit. They have much in common, but most notably, they are failing many of their students.

While there are indeed many good and well-meaning teachers, the mandates from the Fed, unions, and special interest groups have turned public education aside from its original high calling into a boondoggle off which entire sections of society live. And since the actions of the unions have made it nearly impossible to demand results from teachers and administrators, we are seeing many of our schools produce students without basic skills, and the idea of higher education doesn't take these young people any higher.

In recent years there have been a number of employees who come to work for me that have had bachelor's degrees and in some cases master's degrees or higher in areas that have nothing to do with the job they are doing for me. I recall one instance where an employee had spent over four years at a good state university studying sports science management or some such degree. They were assured by the caring professionals at the school that this was a degree program where they would find themselves in demand. Well, four years and $30,000 to $40,000 later, she could not find work, other than "low man on the totem pole" at a local gym, cleaning the locker room. She went on to work at a hotel restaurant and later worked as a receptionist/administrative assistant. Finally, she determined that she would need additional training for a career that actually paid what she had hoped to make.

After enrolling in a two-year program, she learned that most of the math and science she had studied for her first degree did not amount to much, and she would have to take remedial, college-level math and science before beginning her new studies—an unpleasant wake-up call for this young woman who thought her four-year degree would put her on the career path of her choice.

In another instance, a young working man decided to go back and get his college degree. He was dedicated to his goal, but like most college applicants, he had to apply for loans to pay for the education he wanted from a very prestigious school. Four or five years later and over $40,000 in debt, he could not find a job in the field for which he had just spent the greater part of half a decade studying.

These are not isolated cases. We spend thousands, if not tens of thousands, annually to send our children to colleges for liberal arts degrees. As noted in the two previous anecdotes, this can often be for little real gain. Conversely, the thing that made these two people good employees was not their specific training; it was the fact that both of them had worked while going to school, and it was their working experience that motivated me to hire them. The bottom line, really, was that both of these individuals had a good work ethic and knew what it was to work in the real world.

As I look back at some of the best employees I have ever had the pleasure of working with, I am struck by the fact that some of them have had no college-level training at all, but almost every one of them has brought to the table real-world experience, natural intelligence, a good work ethic, and a willingness to learn new things. I am in no way discounting those who have come to work with a college degree or two in hand, but I also want to be clear that does not necessarily give them an advantage over those who have a teachable spirit and a desire to work hard and succeed. Most important to their success has been the love of the work they do, because if you don't like what you do, you will rarely excel in it.

We run one of the largest radio news networks in the country, and some might be surprised to know that our senior engineer who oversees the day-to-day technical operations does NOT have a college degree, but he does have a lot of experience in the broadcast field. He has gained his education in the real world in the field of work that he enjoys. This is a foreign concept to many in this day and age, but apprenticeships were the expected route of learning, up until the middle of the 1900s. Even today most trades involve some apprentice work after technical training to attain the level of experience and wisdom to master a trade or craft.

I have friends who are plumbers and electricians who make very good livings for themselves and their families. We depend on them to fix our plumbing or our electrical outlets when they go on the blink. One of the wealthier men in my community built his electrical contracting company from the ground up. I am sure it has been some time since he was crawling around in an attic wiring a new house, but he started his business from scratch and has been very successful at his trade.

Now, I am not saying that your child's only good options are to be a plumber or electrician and that they should forgo college. But if they want to be productive parts of the community yet discover that college may not be for them, then there is no shame in being a master at a hands-on, technical vocation. I remember the story of a surgeon who was called in the middle of a wintry night to report to the hospital. As he prepared himself to go, he realized the water pipes in his house had frozen, so he quickly called a plumber who came out to his home and within fifteen minutes had fixed his pipes. The plumber promptly handed the surgeon a bill for four hundred dollars. The surgeon was livid and exclaimed that was more than he made as a surgeon for that amount of work. To that, the plumber simply replied, "More than *I* used to make as a surgeon too."

We are often conditioned to believe that our child must pursue a career as a doctor, engineer, lawyer, or some highly noted professional, but the truth is, we all come to the table with certain natural talents and gifts that aid society and make us a living. Hopefully, our talents will provide some measure of happiness as we serve and make a living, but it is not always in the field that society thinks is glamorous. Don't get me wrong: if your child intends to become a physician, he or she will most definitely need the necessary technical and scientific training for their field. The same is true if they are planning to become an electrical or civil engineer or a scientist. Ultimately success has more to do with whether they are using their God-given talents effectively, and just because our nation's educational system is failing to do its job, we as the church and Christian parents are not any less responsible to give them the guidance they need to live out the life God has for them.

Where the Money Goes

If a manufacturer was putting out a product with the defect rate we have coming out of many if not most of our public schools, they would be run out of business. Adding insult to injury, it seems those who fail the biggest get the biggest promotions. Take Arne Duncan, for example. Mr. Duncan formerly held the position of superintendent of the Chicago public school system, a district that is supposed to educate some 400,000 students with an annual budget in excess of $4 billion in taxpayer money.[1] That breaks down to spending more than $10,000 per annum per student, but the results are far from dazzling. Just prior to Mr. Duncan leaving his post in Chicago, a job he held for eight years, the academic achievement tests of eighth-grade students indicated that 83 percent could not read or write at their grade level.[2] It would be easy for most politicians to simply blame the previous administration—but Mr. Duncan had been the superintendent for the entire academic career of these students! His reward for such failure: *Barack Obama made him the U.S. secretary of education!*

Wait; it gets worse. In his capacity as secretary of education, Mr. Duncan has proceeded to gut programs that have been effective, while directing funding to other Obama appointees such as Mr. Kevin Jennings, the "safe schools czar," who is an open homosexual and believes in forcing homocentric sexual education upon children as young as five years old![3]

Additionally, and with the full consent of the president, Duncan was able to make the NEA and the education establishment almost giddy by abolishing one of the most successful programs in the DC school district. What did he do? He closed the vouchers program for underserved students. Under that program, roughly 1,700 DC public-school students were able to take the taxpayer funds that would have been spent in a local public school and apply them instead to the private or parochial school of their choice—including the private school that President Obama's daughters attend.[4]

These 1,700 students who were allowed to escape the public system were excelling in their studies and receiving a much better education than in the public schools. Why? Because the private schools must show results if they intend to stay in business against their competition.

Nevertheless, the program is being shut down, and these students, along with the rest of DC public school students, will be stuck in largely failing, anticompetitive schools that leave them at a terrible disadvantage when they leave school and move into the brutally real world of life and business. The result will likely be another generation of largely dysfunctional, illiterate adults with few prospects of success.

Paying for College: Lottery or Scholarships?

Let's go back to the college level. Many states have created lotteries with the proclaimed intention of funneling the proceeds from gambling into education. Some states, such as Georgia, for instance, started HOPE scholarship programs to enable students to go to college. Not a bad idea, you say? Well, on the surface you would be right, but the reality is, the merit required to receive one of these scholarships was constantly dropped to lower and lower levels of achievement. The result, as you probably guessed, was that it prompted many to attend the state college of their choice, but because they could not make it at that level, many were dropping out within the first year or two of studies. Some simply were not prepared, while others probably should never have been there in the first place. These state-run scholarship programs were creating another false system where students who really did not merit admission were now able to have someone else pay for their education. In the process, it put further burdens on the colleges and universities who were required to spend large sums of money and manpower on remedial education. Additionally, this has led to squandering resources and potential scholarship money that could have gone to real student scholars. Worse yet you have a generation of underachievers who have been pushed to attend college only to waste two years of their life and untold sums of money when they could have been gaining experience in a field where they were more inclined to succeed and become productive, taxpaying citizens.

Of course, the education establishment loved this influx of new dollars, and as a result, they consistently raised tuition and fees. Those receiving the easy scholarship money couldn't care less, because it was not costing them anything. Again, those who merit scholarships or grants increasingly find themselves on the short end of the stick, and those who are working to pay their way through college are hit with ever-increasing levels of tuition and fees. Parents who have children in college or preparing to enter college know all too well how rapidly the cost of college is going up each year. But, as we have pointed out, the end product is not necessarily improving.

Battlefield of the Mind = Battle for Our Nation

Let's look at one final issue with regard to higher education. This area deals with the real battle for the minds of our children—and ultimately our nation. You spend nearly twenty years preparing your children for the realities of the world. We know that the first five years are the most formative and the most important for instilling basic values in our children. Scripture points to this when we read in Proverbs 22:6, "Train up a child in the way he should go, and when he is old he will not depart from it." We take our children to church and introduce them to virtue and morals and teach them right from wrong. As they get older, we take pains to shield them from some of the uglier things in this life, and ultimately we hope they are prepared to stand on their own with the Holy Spirit by their side against the wiles of the enemy. But after all of this, we so often "throw them to lions" in the universities that try every trick in the book to turn their minds away from the precepts we spent nearly two decades instilling in them!

Many college professors are little more than tenured teachers who may have not been able to make it in the private sector. Worse yet, some were merely full-time students who never left college, and the world of academia is all they know. Some are pseudo sophisticated intellectuals who, like the grasshopper, climbed the tallest blade of grass and proclaimed he had seen the world. This has a tendency to breed a kind of academic club where both pride and fear box many into a vicious cycle of theory and thought that can be far outside the norm—and often, far removed from the truth.

Consider the global-warming scam that is being debunked around the world today, and yet it was taught as "fact" and "truth" for an appalling number of years. Unfortunately, this kind of intellectual dishonesty is often foisted upon your children as education.

Does your son or daughter have the discernment to know the difference or to dissect the professor's arguments? On the farm we call it "eating the hay and spitting out the sticks." Can they rightly discern the truth? Of course they are at an immediate disadvantage as the professors wander the grounds of the institutions as near-gods who dispense the grades that determine the student's success. Tick them off or disagree with them and you may fail their class.

I remember a Western civilization course I had to take in my undergraduate degree. On the first day of class the teacher told us that she was certain that all history indicated that we had always been a matriarchal society until the last thousand years; as a result, men were essentially the root cause of almost all problems in the world. Some introduction, huh? We were given two grades for the semester that included a midterm essay-type test and an end-of-term paper on a historical figure. I studied diligently for the midterm (I was paying for school out of my own pocket, working full-time as I went to college), but despite my efforts, I was given a C on the test. It seemed the instructor did not like some of my answers, despite the fact they were historically accurate. I figured I would have to get an A on the paper just to come out with a B for the class. So, I prayed about the subject of the paper, and I believe the Lord gave me the perfect historical figure and title for the assignment: "Esther: A Woman Who Led a Nation." I did not bow to the teacher's concept of history; instead, I wrote a historically accurate piece on a figure from the Bible, with additional backing from modern textbooks regarding Esther's husband, the Persian King Xerxes. What do you know! She gave me an A for the paper—and somehow, an A for the semester! Thankfully, I had the discernment to know that much of what this person was teaching was utter hogwash, but many in the class did not, and they took it all in as educational gospel. This happens daily on college campuses across the nation.

If you dare to challenge evolution, you had better be prepared for the wrath of the professors. Further, if you value virtue, morals, and common sense, you had better expect quite the opposite from many of the faculty.

Sadly we are losing many young people from the faith as a result of the indoctrination of some college campus. I believe it was George Barna who produced a study indicating that after four years at a university, 70 percent of Christian young adults left the faith they had known all of their lives.[5] I am a member of the Gideon organization and as such have the opportunity to pass out pocket-sized copies of the New Testament, Psalms, and Proverbs at the local university from time to time. The difference in the reception we receive from the students between the fall term and the spring term never ceases to amaze me. In the fall, the freshman are just coming onto campus and are happy to receive a New Testament from the fellows handing them out and wishing them a good day. By the time spring comes around and the professors have had the students' minds captive for hours daily, the response to the Bible distribution becomes decidedly cool and tepid—sometimes outright hostile. We also know from various surveys that our young men and women are more likely than not to give in to sex outside of marriage while at college. As a matter of fact, fewer than 20 percent of young men and women are still virgins after they leave college and one in four has a sexually transmitted disease!

Once again, I want to emphasize that I am not against education, but I think we all need to understand the realities of many of the modern-day institutions that often masquerade as places of higher learning. We need to give careful consideration to the matter, discussing with our children whether they want to attend college or simply begin their own careers or businesses. We all know friends whose children have bucked the trend and gone out on their own after high school and made something of their lives without a college degree. For crying out loud, Bill Gates is a college dropout!

On a serious note, far too much damage is being done to our children and our society from much of the liberal arts education that we are paying for today. We must take a step back and really weigh the benefits as well as the detriments of sending our children to college. If in the end you determine it is necessary for the field they are choosing for a career, I urge you to give much prayer to considering what schools they will apply to. Thankfully there are a few schools that will not openly and viciously attack your son's or daughter's belief system, but they are the exception rather than the norm.

Think twice before spending your money and potentially sacrificing your children and their salvation in sending them to college. For additional background on the all-out assault for the minds of our children on the college campus, do an Internet search for the writings of Mike Adams, a professor who came to Christ late in life and is a conservative now. His battles for freedom of thought on the campus and the retaliation he has received for it is amazing.

And on a final note, don't be afraid to make your child a financial partner in his or her education. Good banks don't make 100 percent loans anymore. They require the loan applicant to have a larger down payment these days, and for good reason, they want the borrower to have "skin in the game," as it makes them more likely to perform on the loan. The same is true with parents and their college students. The son or daughter needs to understand the costs. It will aid them in transitioning into adulthood and the real world. While my folks had the ability to send me to college, they allowed me the opportunity to pay my own way (they paid for the first semester, which was the worst). But then a funny thing happened. I had a vested interest to make sure the dollars *I* had worked so hard for and handed over to the university were being well spent. I didn't want *my* dollars to be wasted!

It was a great lesson and one for which I am grateful to my parents. It allowed me to get some great, real-world experience that was later very beneficial in my career work. Believe me, it won't kill your kid either. They just think it will.

WHY ONLY A PARTIAL "LOAF"?

I N CONCLUSION, LET ME REITERATE THE FACT THAT THE gospel is an economic, political, and spiritual message of kingdom principles. We have covered all of those areas in preceding chapters. So why, then, do we not receive teachings regarding all of those things in various "religious" settings?

The Catholics, Anglicans, Episcopalians, and Lutherans do a great job in liturgical expression and symbolism of the church. Evangelicals are excellent in evangelistic outreach and proclaiming John 3:16. The "health and wealth gospel" movement is diligent in proclaiming Proverbs 13:22: "A good man leaveth an inheritance to his children's children: and the wealth of the sinner is laid up for the just" (KJV). You just have to give to one of their ministries with your "seed faith" offering to tap into the wealth. Do we really believe that God in His infinite wisdom will burden anyone with massive new wealth if they don't understand how the system works?

Friends, you can't just name it and claim it. You can't just put a fish and a cross on the world system and call it of God. You can't just wear your favorite Christian jewelry and expect total protection from the evils in the world system, and you can't just show up at your favorite house of worship and get equipped for what is facing us, UNLESS you are being instructed in the whole counsel of God by wise leadership.

Our main job in this period of crisis is to raise up wisdom in a couple of generations that lack wisdom. If you are a pastor or church leader who is fully engaged in the culture war, keep up the good fight. If you are a pastor or church leader not fully engaged in the culture war, stop "eating" the "sheep," and start feeding the sheep. These will be tough times but exciting times. We've read the back of "the book," and "we win."

NOTES

Introduction

1. William Wirt Henry and Bert Franklin, *Patrick Henry: Life, Correspondence and Speeches*, volume 1 (New York: Ortis Publishing, 1891, 1969).

Chapter 1
Most Won't Say It, but You Should Know

1. Frédéric Bastiat, *The Law* (Irvington-on-Hudson, NY: Foundation for Economic Education, 1995), 5.

2. Alexander Fraser Tyler, as quoted in *Monetary & Economic Review* (published by First American Monetary Consultants, Ft. Collins, CO), January 1992, 6.

3. Thomas Hoenig, speech titled "Pew-Peterson Commission on Budget Reform" (*Financial Times*, London), February 16, 2010.

4. Chris W. Bell, "King Had a Dream, but Blacks Now Face a Nightmare," published with author's permission in *Unravelling The New World Order*, (Fort Collins, CO: First American Monetary Consultants), February 18, 2010.

5. Ibid.

6. Ibid.

7. Jessica Ravitz, "Out-of-Wedlock Births Hit Record High," CNN.com, April 8, 2009, http://www.cnn.com/2009/LIVING/wayof life/04/08/out.of.wedlock.births/index.html (accessed March 29, 2010).

8. Dennis Cauchon, "For Feds, More Get 6-Figure Salaries," USAToday.com, December 11, 2009, http://www.usatoday.com/news/ washington/2009-12-10-federal-pay-salaries_N.htm (accessed March 30, 2010).

9. Ibid.

10. Ceridian-UCLA Pulse of Commerce Index, January 2010.

11. Paul Wiseman, "Trucking Index Forecasts Gloom," *USA Today*, February 10, 2010, 1B.

12. Julie Crenshaw, "Laffer: Obama Budget Is Plan for Catastrophe," *Money News, NewsMax.com*, February 20, 2010.

13. Ibid.

14. Ibid.

15. Ibid.

16. Ari Levey and Carol Zimmer, "California Hotels Go Green With Low-flow Toilets, Solar Lights," Bloomberg.com, April 27, 2007, http://www.bloomberg.com/apps/news?pid=20670001&sid =afIESX3LdgnQ (accessed March 22, 2010).

17. "Poll: 1 in 4 U.S. Young Muslims OK With Homicide Bombings Against Civilians," FoxNews.com, May 23, 2007, http://www.foxnews.com/story/0,2933,274934,00.html (accessed March 22, 2010).

18. "Kenyan-born Obama All Set for U.S. Senate," FreeRepublic .com, October 15, 2009, http://www.freerepublic.com/focus/news/ 2362801/posts (accessed March 22, 2010).

19. Ibid.

20. Ibid.

21. Ben Stein, "We've Figured Him Out," *The American Spectator*, Arlington, Virginia, July 24, 2009.

22. *Oxford English Dictionary*, 568–569, s.v. "religio."

23. Richard Owen, "Chief Exorcist Father Gabriele Amorth Says Devil Is in the Vatican," TimesOnline.com, March 11, 2010, http://www.timesonline.co.uk/tol/comment/faith/article7056689.ece (accessed March 22, 2010).

24. Ibid.

25. Ibid.

Chapter 2
Money Answereth All Things

1. *Webster's New World Dictionary*, Third College Edition, s.v. "money."

2. Ibid., s.v. "inflation."

Chapter 3
"Faith-Based" Money

1. Roger Sherman, *A Caveat Against Injustice* (Boring, OR: CPA Book Publisher, 1999).

2. Eagan Caesar Corti, *The Rise of the House of Rothschild* (Belmont, MA: Blue Ribbon Books, 1971), 8.

3. Aldo Svaldi, "Co-creator of the Euro Offers Terra," *Denver Post*, October 24, 2003, 1C.

4. Ibid.

5. Ibid.

6. Alan Greenspan in testimony before U.S. Congress, June 14, 2004.

7. Henry Hazlitt, "Inflation in One Page," published in *The Freeman*, May 1978.

8. Ibid.

Chapter 4
The Coming Financial Wipeout

1. Brett Arends, "Economic 'Armageddon' Predicted," *Boston Herald*, November 23, 2004, http://www.fromthewilderness.com/free/ ww3/112304_economic_armageddon.shtml (accessed April 1, 2010).

2. Stephen Roach, "Economic Armageddon?" *Monetary and Economic Review*, Fall/Winter 2004, 8.

3. Thomas Sowell, "Poverty and the Left," Townhall.com, December 1, 2000, http://townhall.com/columnists/ThomasSowell/ 200/12/01/poverty_and_the_left (accessed March 23, 2010).

4. John Maynard Keynes, *The Economic Consequences of the Peace* (New York: Harcourt Brace, 1920), 148–149.

Chapter 5
Simple Financial Solutions (Part 1)

1. The Survey of Consumer Payment Choice, Federal Reserve Bank of Boston, January 2010; Ben Woolsey and Matt Schulz, "Credit Card Statistics, Industry Facts, Debt, Statistics," Creditcards.com, March 19, 2010, http://www.creditcards.com/credit-card-news/ credit-card-industry-facts-personal-debt-statistics-1276.php (accessed March 29, 2010).

2. Liz Pulliam Weston, "The Truth About Credit Card Debt," MSN.com, http://moneycentral.msn.com/content/Banking/ creditcardsmarts/P74808.asp (accessed March 29, 2010).

3. "Despite Fewer Offers Than Previous Years. As of 2008 There Were Over 1.34 Billion in US," WashingtonPost.com, November 16, 2008.

Chapter 6
Simple Financial Solutions (Part 2)

1. IRN/USA News, "News and Views: Richard L. Scott Interview," radio broadcast, January 25, 2010.

Chapter 8
Government and the Economy

1. John Maynard Keynes, *The Economic Consequences of the Peace*, (London: McMillan/St. Martin's Press for the Royal Economic Society, 1919, 1920, 1971), 148–149.
2. Ibid.
3. Ron Paul, "Government Policy and False Prosperity," *Texas Straight Talk*, January 27, 2003, www.house.gov/paul/tst (accessed March 25, 2010).
4. Ibid.
5. Ibid.

Chapter 9
Big Government; Small Economy

1. Dennis Lockhart, speech to Chamber of Commerce, Chattanooga, TN, Agence France Presse (AFP), August, 26, 2009.
2. Ibid.
3. Lawrence H. Summers, "Unemployment," The Concise Encyclopedia of Economics, http://www.econlib.org/library/Enc/Unemployment.html (accessed March 30, 2010).
4. Cauchon, "For Feds, More Get 6-Figure Salaries."
5. Keynes, *The Economic Consequence of the Peace*.
6. Budget of the United States Government, Fiscal Year 2011, Office of Management and Budget, Washington DC, http://www.gpoaccess.gov/usbudget/fy11/index.html (accessed March 30, 2010).
7. Jody Shenn, "'Underwater' Mortgages to Hit 48%, Deutsche Bank Says," Bloomberg.com, http://www.bloomberg.com/apps/news?pid=20603037&sid=adBYDzUMt68k (accessed March 30, 2010).
8. Al Yon, "About Half of U.S. Mortgages Seen Underwater by 2011," Reuters.com, http://www.reuters.com/article/idUS-TRE5745JP20090805 (accessed March 30, 2010).

Chapter 10
Where's the Struggle?

1. Alfred Frazer Tyler, quoted in *Monetary & Economic Review*, pub. Ft. Collins, CO, January 1992, 6.

Chapter 11
Rhetoric vs. Reality

1. Lindsay Renick Mayer, "Update: Fannie Mae and Freddie Mac Invest in Lawmakers," OpenSecrets.com: Center for Responsive Politics, September 11, 2008, http://www.opensecrets.org/news/2008/09/update-fannie-mae-and-freddie.html (accessed March 30, 2010).

2. Nick Loris, "CBO Grossly Underestimates Costs of Cap and Trade," The Heritage Foundation, July 22, 2009, http://blog.heritage.org/2009/06/22/cbo-grossly-underestimates-costs-of-cap-and-trade/ (accessed March 30, 2010).

3. Ed Barnes, "Obama Draws Fire for Appointing SEIU's Stern to Deficit Panel," FoxNews.com, March 6, 2010, http://www.foxnews.com/politics/2010/03/05/obama-draws-appointing-seius-stern-deficit-panel/ (accessed March 30, 2010).

Chapter 12
Media Takeover

1. "CyberAlert Extra: Wednesday Night Dan Rather Discovered Chandra Levy, but Only to Clear Condit, Who Was Not Labeled a Democrat, and Impugn DC Police," Media Research Council 113, no. 6 (July 18, 2001), http://www.mrc.org/cyberalerts/2001/cyb20010718_extra.asp#1 (accessed March 30, 2010).

2. Associated Press, "Sen. Vitter Apologizes for Number Showing Up on Phone Records of Alleged Prostitution Ring," FOXNews.com, http://www.foxnews.com/story/0,2933,288740,00.html (access March 30, 2010); Stephen W. Smith, "Vitter Back in Senate Amid Sex Scandal," CBS.com, July 17, 2007, http://www.cbsnews.com/stories/2007/07/17/politics/main3066211.shtml (accessed March 30, 2010).

3. John Mercurio, "Lott Apologizes for Thurmond Comment," CNN.com, http://archives.cnn.com/2002/ALLPOLITICS/12/09/lott.comment/ (accessed March 30, 2010).

4. Bruce Drake, "Reid Apologizes for Racial Remark About Obama, and Also Sinks in a Poll," InsidePoliticsDaily.com, http://www.politicsdaily.com/2010/01/09/reid-apologizes-for-racial-remark-about-obama-and-also-sinks-in/ (accessed April 1, 2010).

5. Brent Baker, "ABC, CBS & NBC Verdict: Obama's Stimulus a Success," Newsbusters.org, February 17, 2010, http://newsbusters.org/blogs/brent-baker/2010/02/17/abc-cbs-and-nbc-verdict-obamas-stimulus-success-cbs-frets-public-refuse (accessed March 30, 2010).

6. Bureau of Labor Statistics, Unemployment figures for December 2009, January 2010, February 2010, http://www.bls.gov/ (accessed March 30, 2010).

7. "Patrick Henry Quotes," BrainyQuote.com, http://www.brainyquote.com/quotes/quotes/p/patrickhen165618.html (accessed March 26, 2010).

Chapter 13
Commit and Occupy

1. John R. Lott, *More Guns, Less Crime: Understanding Crime and Gun-Control Laws*, (Chicago, IL: University of Chicago, 1997).

2. Charl Van Wyk, *Shooting Back: The Right and Duty of Self Defense* (Capetown, South Africa: Christian Liberty Books, 2001).

3. Charles C. Ryrie, *Ryrie Study Bible* (Chicago, IL: Moody Publishers, 1986).

4. Ibid.

Chapter 14
Give Me Liberty

1. David Paul Kuhn, "Exit Polls: How Obama Won," Politico.com, http://www.politico.com/news/stories/1108/15297.html (accessed April 1, 2010).

2. Jill Stanek, "Born Alive Infants Protection Act," interview on News & Views Fall of 2008; Mark Halperin "After Saddleback, Obama Gets Heated With Brody," FreeRepublic.com, August 16, 2008, http://www.freerepublic.com/focus/f-news/2063182/posts (accessed March 30, 2010).

3. BBC Report, "Obama Condemns Israel at UN," March 14, 2010; Israeli Army Radio interview with Hagai Ben Artzi, brother-in-law to Israeli Prime Minister Benjamin Netanyahu, March 17, 2010.

4. "Barack Obama on Gun Control," OnTheIssues.com, http://www.ontheissues.org/Barack_Obama.htm#Gun_Control (accessed March 30, 2010).

Chapter 16
What Happened to the Fathers?

1. Ronald Kessler, *Inside the White House* (Chicago, IL: Simon & Schuster, 1996), 33.

2. Jonah Goldberg, *Liberal Fascism: The Secret History of the American Left* (New York: Doubleday, 2008).

3. Bureau of Labor Statistics, Unemployment figures for December 2009, January 2010, February 2010, http://www.bls.gov/ (accessed March 30, 2010).

4. Walter Williams, "How Not to Be Poor," *Capitalism* magazine, May 11, 2005, http://www.capmag.com/article.asp?ID=4223 (accessed March 29, 2010).

5. National Religious Broadcasters Conference, Anaheim, CA, 2005

Chapter 17
The Battle for Your Child's Mind and Soul

1. Chicago Public Schools FY2007 Operating Budget ($4.669 billion); Chicago Public Schools Student Profiles 2000–2008 (Avg. Student Population 432,328). Divide budget by total number of students to get estimated spending per student education at $10,807 per annum.

2. Gregory Hinz, "Chicago Public School Reform Flops," ChicagoBusiness.com, June 30, 2009, http://www.chicagobusiness.com/cgi-bin/blogs/hinz.pl?plckController=Blog&plckScript=blogscrip t&plckElementId=blogdest&plckBlogPage=BlogViewPost&plckPostId =Blog%3A1daca073-2eab-468e-9f19-ec177090a35cPost%3A879511e5-2769-4a3b-87ef-f5958aa29597&sid=sitelife.chicagobusiness .com (accessed March 30, 2010); Matt Hadro, "Education Secretary Nominee Defends Chicago Schools," CNSNews.com, January 14, 2009, http://www.cnsnews.com/news/print/41932 (accessed March 30, 2010).

3. "How He Pushed the Homosexual Agenda to Kids in American Schools," MassResistance.org, September 13, 2009, http://

www.massresistance.org/docs/gen/09d/kevin_jennings/kevinjennings
.html (accessed March 30, 2010).

4. Peter Roff, "Obama Wrong on D.C. School Vouchers," US
News & World Report, April 22, 2009; Interview with Bishop Harry
R. Jackson, Sr., *News and Views* radio program, IRN/USA News,
January, 2010; Interview with Connie Lawn, senior White House
correspondent, *News and Views* radio program, IRN/USA News.

5. Voddie T. Baucham, *Family Driven Faith: Doing What it
Takes to Raise Sons and Daughters Who Walk with God* (n.p.:
Crossway Books, 2007).

INDEX

P